The Fire of Hope, From Victim to Victor
bellaviewater.com
rosephan.com

T. Allen Hanes Publishing Group
www.tAllenHanesPublishingGroup.com
7440 Highway 6, Hitchcock, Texas 77583

ISBN: 978-1-936839-16-2

Testimonials

"Rose Phan's book, The Fire of Hope, is an inspirational story of faith, compassion, family and love. Rose shares her story beautifully and vividly so that we see the over-arching wisdom of perseverance, 'where there is a will, there is a way."

Do yourself a favor, and indulge in this book of life and love.

-Ruth Klein, Soul-Centered Brand Strategist and Productivity Coach Best-selling Author of Time Management for Working Women

"From a Vietnamese boat refugee to a U.S. citizen who embodies the American dream and appreciates the land of opportunities comes a riveting must-read. The real-life stories that leap from the pages of Fire of Hope will captivate your attention and warm your heart. This book is a light of hope and guidance to a struggling humanity."

-Sharon Frame, Former CNN Anchor/Writer

"Rose Phan has written a FIVE-STAR book! From beginning to end you will be taught, inspired, and motivated to overcome your personal obstacles and live a better life. Like the Phoenix, she rose from danger and devastation to become a beacon of hope and a light for others. Rose shines brightly as an author, as a leader, and as an example of what is possible when you have the fire of hope in your heart. I give this book two enthusiastic thumbs up!"

-Dr. Paula Fellingham, Founder/CEO of the Women's Information Network

"The Fire of Hope is a must-have book with "Phantastic" insights and profound secrets for women, men, and teenagers. Through her story of her harrowing journey from communist Vietnam to her new life in the States to her return to Vietnam forty years later, she shows you how she went from victim to victor, rising from the ashes like a phoenix, and how you can do it, too.

This book gives hope that everyone can find meaning and power through their suffering. For the greatest suffering is to believe that one's suffering has no meaning. It is a book of genius and inspiration."

"This book is a light of hope and guidance to a struggling humanity. I would be honored to use it as a text book at the Nerenberg legacy therapy institute."

-Dr. Arnold Nerenberg

"Rose Phan has had an extraordinary life, and her memoir beautifully captures her dramatic escape from Vietnam as a child, her life in a refugee camp, and her success as a businesswoman, wife and mother. She's one who has done it all, and she shows you the principles of living that helped her survive and thrive. When you've escaped an authoritarian regime that took over your country, been stranded on a boat without water or gasoline, been captured and threatened to be returned to torture and death, you have to have the courage to risk everything. Fabulous book! You won't be able to put it down!"

-Chellie Campbell, author of The Wealthy Spirit and Zero to Zillionaire

"Extraordinary story of survival against impossible odds. A true rag to riches story – a must read for everyone.

-Nina Hershberger, CEO Megabucks Marketing, Inc.

"Most of us go through life barely paying attention. Oh, we might pick up a few "life lessons" that we will tell our kids about until they are bored to tears. But how many of us really learned what life had to teach? Rose Phan is one of those remarkable people who paid attention in the class of life experience, and what experiences she has had.

Imagine going from wealth to poverty and then building a successful company that leads you back to wealth. Imagine the need to escape the country of your birth by sneaking out on a dangerous voyage, and needing to fight off armed soldiers to win your freedom. This is just the beginning of Rose's life journey.

At each stage, Rose picked up important lessons that she is eager to share with us. She offers reflections on her experience, a principle she draws from that experience, and action steps that we can take to benefit and learn from her life lessons. The Fire of Hope, from Victim to Victor, is much more than an autobiography. It is a book of lessons for those who seek to overcome the challenges in their own lives. It is unique in its understanding that there are real moral truths, and that it is struggle sometimes to live those truths.

Rose is candid about the struggles she faced. In this book, she offers you the opportunity to walk with her through her experiences and her hard-won wisdom. This is a journey well worth your time. You may not face the challenges Rose encountered in her life (God willing!), but you will still benefit from her experience and the lessons she has learned. Everyone will find something in this book of value. Take the time to journey with Rose and reflect with her as she looks back on what has happened thus far. I can't wait for the sequel she will be able to write as she continues to build on these experiences."

-Tom Caso, Attorney and Law Professor at Chapman University

Preface

In honor of my father's love, sacrifice, and courage, I, the Phoenix-Rose, was determined to write this book. I'm forever grateful for my father's bravery; it saved many lives, including mine. His unselfish love and courage, his willingness to die for his loved ones and for a good cause, and his will of steel left me with a legacy of love, determination, and loyalty to family that will be passed down for many generations.

With so much abundance in America, sometimes we tend to forget the suffering and hardships that still exist around us, or to acknowledge how many blessings we have. Even our own children can lose a sense of drive, because they have never experienced such hardships. Reminding them of the challenges their ancestors endured so they can enjoy their current benefits of comfort and luxury will help them remember to be grateful, to appreciate, and to live meaningful lives.

We need to count our blessings, to savor every moment, and to acknowledge the needs of others. We can make a difference, even in a small way, every day. It starts with thoughts of kindness and the will to carry them out.

This book is meant to help people of all ages appreciate life in the different phases of their journey—whether personal growth or entrepreneurship—in a physical, mental, and spiritual way.

This book covers my journey of discovery in life, business, and relationships.

It is how I discovered the truth of which Emily Dickson wrote: Hope is the thing with feathers that perches in the soul, / that sings the song without words and never stops at all.

Where there is a will, there is a way. There is a solution to every problem, so don't give up in any circumstance. As long as your heart moves you to do the highest good, the universe is there for you. Faith will carry you through any challenge you may encounter in life.

Acknowledgements

In 1976, my first English composition teacher at Saddleback College, a junior college in Mission Viejo, California, kept me after class. One of our assignments was to write a paper. Mine was titled, "There is a Will, there is a Way," and it detailed my escape from communist Vietnam and quest for freedom. She told me that I needed to take my paper and turn it into a book. I agreed, if only to leave the inspiring messages for my children and many generations to come, and to those who want to find courage and appreciation for a meaningful life.

After 40 years, that book is finally becoming a reality. I owe so much to my father, King Win, to my mother, and so many kind people who've helped me in many ways on my journey to this point:

Madeleine Gough, who has been there for me since I started playing the pipe organ at the Old Mission Church in San Juan Capistrano shortly after stepping foot in California

Mrs. Nakyong Chai, head of the Music Department of Saddleback College, who helped me discover my inner self through my piano playing

Mrs. Mary Campbell, my college classmate who first taught me about positive thinking

John Cox, an attorney and friend who always lends an ear without judgment, and was the first person who gave me the book *Men are from Mars, Women are from Venus* by John Gray

Reverend Peter Minh Quang Chu, a PhD in Psychology who is the founder of the Vietnamese Marriage Family Enrichment Program and has taught me to be a deeper, more effective family counselor

Joseph Bao and Phuoc Do, my godparents, who were our guardian angels and counselors

Dr. Arnold Nerenberg, whom I quote throughout this book and who shares his wisdom and support/

And, most of all, with gratitude, my faithful and supportive husband, Minh Phan, and my three wonderful caring sons, Justin, Joshua, and Jesse Phan, who have made my life complete and meaningful. I am grateful for their presence in my life.

Introduction

After the fall of South Vietnam in 1975 and the subsequent creation of the Republic of Vietnam, many who fought against the North during the actual war feared retribution from the communist government. Rightfully so, as it has been estimated that 65,000 Vietnamese were executed after the end of the war. In addition, some 1 million were sent to prison/re-education camps, where another estimated 165,000 died; and an additional 1 million were sent to reclaim and farm land in the jungle. In Ho Chi Minh City (formally Saigon), seen as a bastion of "Americanization," rules were repressive and traditional freedoms were few.

Many chose to leave the country, but under Communist rule, this was illegal. This made air travel from Vietnam out of the question, leaving only makeshift boats or fishing boats as escape options. These types of boats were not built for open waters. Couple this with overcrowding and they became an extremely dangerous, and potentially lethal, way to travel on the open seas.

No one can be sure how many people fled, although some experts estimate as many as 2 million. Estimates for the number of people who lost their lives varies from 50,000 to 200,000, according to the Australian Immigration Ministry. The primary cause of death was drowning, though many refugees were attacked by pirates and murdered or sold into slavery and prostitution.

Even if boat people did manage to land, some countries in the region, such as Malaysia, turned those people away. Refugees deliberately sank their boats offshore to stop authorities from towing them back out to sea. Many refugees ended up settling in the United States and Europe. The U.S. accepted 823,000 refugees; Britain accepted 19,000; France accepted 96,000; and Australia and Canada accepted 137,000 each.

Table of Contents

1

Family

Before I begin my escape story, I'd like to tell you about my father, who was called King Win. He was born in a poor family and had two older brothers. One was single and alcoholic; the other was married with a large family—how many children, I'm not sure. My father didn't receive much schooling. Instead, he had to work hard at a very young age as an errand boy for a wealthy family that owned multiple businesses. He grew up learning everything by himself in his surroundings. Luckily, some senior business people took him under their wings and guided him. Starting out as a nobody, he rose to become a wealthy businessman with the capability to provide his family with an above-average living: a nice house, cars, maids, a chauffeur, and private school for his children. He was an entrepreneur who earned great respect from the business world in the South of Vietnam.

How my father met and courted my mom, I'm not sure, but his passion won her heart when she was a very young girl.

Mom used to say, "Your dad told me that he'd die if he couldn't marry me. I was afraid of him dying because of me."

How silly was that? How passionate my father must've been to conquer the woman of his life! But it was fate. After all, they became husband and wife.

My father wasn't a large man —about five feet tall—but he had a big temper and an equally big heart, and would risk his life to protect his family. One time years ago when my mom and we kids were standing in line to get tickets for a movie, a man behind my mother tried to steal money from her pocket. My father grabbed the thief and beat him up. Despite his size, he was a powerful man, mentally and physically.

My mom was an excellent student in high school, even though she lost her mother when she was only six years old. Raised by her father and grandmother, she had a sister who was older by two years, a four-year-old brother, and her youngest sister, who was two years old.

Mom was beautiful and softhearted, but very shy. , and her in-laws abused her. They were so cruel that I grew up resenting my paternal grandmother and had hate-filled nightmares. She dedicated her life to her five children, and was neither a clever wife nor a social person. When my father started to hustle his business and climb the social ladder, she was shy and jealous that he attended social events without her and was surrounded by women. Her resentment drove a wedge between them. The more resentment she had, the more sins my father committed. The more tears Mom shed, the more anger I had toward my dad, and later, toward all men. It made me very fearful about any relationship. I grew very suspicious and cautious, questioning everything and everyone. I lived in a shell, channeling my energies into learning and family, and I rarely socialized.

I remembered how miserable my mom used to be, even after her financial condition later improved due to my father's success. He made it through many challenges and hardships with hard work and courage. Yes, he was aggressive, but he was also creative and extraordinary. He knew when to fight for what was important, but he also knew when to swallow his pride and yield. I admired his guts in standing up to protect his family and friends. He was very generous and kind in helping the weak in many different ways.

Being the oldest child and a girl (to accompany him at many banquets and social events when I was in high school. I observed how he acted and reacted and how he treated and was treated by good and bad people. I learned that life is not always easy and fair and how one should behave in order to survive with honor or just to survive to be ahead of the game. He wanted to give us the best education, an education he didn't have, and my mom was open to spending money for our education, including private courses and tuition to the most privileged school in the city of Saigon. My parents wanted to give us the best of everything, as most loving parents would.

So, I was fortunate to go to a French Catholic private school called Regina Mundi (Queen of the World), also known as "Couvent des Oiseaux" (Convent of the Birds). This was a school for children from wealthy and socially prominent families.

My maternal grandfather came from a high-ranking, wealthy, official Chinese family who sent him to France to study. When he came back to China, they expected him to be in politics, but he chose a completely opposite path, which was to follow Jesus Christ as a devoted Catholic. In the face of his parents' disappointment, he left China for Vietnam and made a living as a French business interpreter and consultant. He married and had four children but lost his wife at a very young age, remained a bachelor, and raised his family with a very strict approach. . He liked to tell stories about his experiences, his faith, and his wisdom.

While growing up, I used to be afraid of him and his strictness, but I learned to appreciate all of the values and wisdom he left with us. He taught us many things, such as holding chopsticks properly, good manners at the table and when talking and listening, the smart way to savor our food and life with gratitude, the best position when writing and how to study properly, tips to protect our eyesight gratitude for nature, and valuing all given to us by God. They were valuable lessons to me, even though I didn't realize these as a kid. Most of all, he used to call me "my little princess" when he saw me playing the piano.

My grandfather was a faithful Christ follower. He made a lot of money but gave away a lot to many in need. At the end of his life, his most treasured possession was a thick diary that had a cross for every chapter. It was not just a cross, but on each corner of the cross, there was something written: date, place, time, and the person he was writing about. It seemed that the memories and experiences were more precious to him than all of the wealth and assets he owned.

He was far from ordinary in many ways. I never saw him drive a car, even though I assumed he could afford it. After he retired, he walked everywhere, so much so that thick varicose veins bulged in his legs.

His hair was the length of Jesus' hair, and everywhere he went, he praised the Lord for the air he breathed, the trees, the flowers, and everything around him. He was very conscious and particular of how everything would or should be. Yes, he was strict but kind-hearted at the same time. I wondered how he could be both things at the same time, if it was because Jesus could be both, too; I could only speculate about that.

Above all, my grandfather was a great example of gratitude.

~ ~ ~

Reflections

My family tree is not in any way perfect—nor are most families. I confess that there were times I wished I'd been born into royalty, or with parents who had more education, and a wealthier social status, especially when I compared them with some of my classmates.

On the surface, this might sound funny. And I knew I was more fortunate than many orphans who would have been happy with any family at all, such as a mother, father, brother, sister, or cousin. Over the years I've realized I was luckier than a lot of the unfortunate, and I'm grateful for that.

Our ideas and attitudes generate our emotional responses. For example, if I see myself as a worthless person, I may experience many painful and persistent emotions— discouragement, depression, sadness, and maybe even suicidal feelings. But if I can be brought to realize by the affirming and unconditional love of another that I am really a decent and lovable person of considerable worth, this whole pattern changes radically. As my distorted perception is corrected, is I will be gradually transformed into a self-confident, assured, and happy person. Thus, when I saw the positive side of having a family I learned to accept what I had with gratitude, instead of with false expectations or disappointment.

Rose's Principle #1: Accept with Gratitude

Accept your roots and embrace them with gratitude. Your parents may not be perfect or even the way you expect or want them to be, but be grateful that you have parents and family who care.

Be honest and recognize the truth—the bad *and* the good. Be wise and learn from their mistakes, shortcomings, and weaknesses. Be brave and be authentic. Most of all, be grateful and honor your elders, including but not limited to your parents and grandparents. One cannot grow peacefully unless one honors and accepts the truth of one's origins.

My own experience, with myself and with others, leads me to believe that a change in undesirable emotional patterns can come only with a change in thinking—with a change in one's perception of reality or vision. It now seems obvious to me that our emotional reactions are not permanent parts of our makeup. Rather, they grow out of the way we see ourselves, other people, life, the world, and God. Our perceptions become the habitual frame of reference within which we act and react. In the pursuit of the fullness of human life, everything depends on this frame of reference, this habitual outlook, this basic vision which I have of myself, others, life, the world, and God. What we see is what we get.

Exercise Action Steps:

After waking up every morning, the first thing I usually do is pound and rub each arm and each leg with the fist of the opposite hand. As a Catholic, I make the Sign of the Cross to thank God for being alive, but if you prefer, you can just take a moment to reflect on three things that you are grateful for. I usually look over to my side to be grateful that my husband is well. The second thing I am grateful for is that my children are all healthy. The third thing I am grateful for is that I am looking forward to my things to do that day.

Every morning, I always count at least three things that I am grateful for and thank God for keeping me safe. I want to be fully human and fully alive. I promise myself that I will do my best to be productive, starting with drinking a large glass of alkaline water before doing my exercise.

The most fulfilling and transforming moments I've experienced have been moments of "insights." Sometimes these precious insights explode on me like the Fourth of July. Sometimes, they come like the dawn, slowly and gradually bestowing a gift of light and life. The most meaningful moments of my own life were the moments of faith, hope, love, and insight (*Man in Search of a Soul*). Through the eyes of our minds, you and I look out at reality (ourselves and other people, life, the world and God). However, we see things differently. That's what makes each of us unique.

2

Private Boarding School

When I was young (from about first until fifth grade), my mom put us in a French school. She couldn't teach us because she'd attended Chinese school and didn't feel qualified. So, my sister and I attended a private boarding school. She hired a widowed teacher for extra tutoring and discipline. Our private teacher lived in a two-bedroom studio on the fourth floor of a building that overlooked Lê Loi, a major street in Saigon. We kept a strict daily schedule. Every morning at 6:30 a.m., we prayed before breakfast, then left with her in a tri-wheel carriage. A man in the back pedaled us to the private Catholic elementary school, where classes started at 8:00 a.m.

We returned to her studio for lunch and took a short nap, then got ready to go back to school from 4:00 p.m. to 6:00 p.m. with her on the same tri-wheeler. After having dinner, we did our homework, with tutoring help from the teacher. A maid cooked and cleaned the house every day. We went home every Friday night for the weekend and returned to the boarding school Sunday evening.

Sometimes, after homework was completed, we were allowed to play with our doll. This was a special doll. She had her own bed with a light bulb on top of the headboard. There were some drawers underneath the bed. The doll had her own clothes to dress up in, and her eyes could blink, depending on what position we put her in. Her eyes stayed open if she was sitting or standing and closed when she was put to "sleep." We called her Bella, and she was the most beautiful doll I'd ever seen. If we didn't play with Bella, we could sit on the balcony and look out at the streets full of cars and pedestrians before going to sleep.

I remember there were times when we saw our father's car driving by. We'd call his name, but the car never stopped. It saddened us that our dad didn't hear us, and we'd cry. We'd have to wait until Friday evening to be picked up to go home.

I don't know how much all of this cost our parents, but I realize now that I was very fortunate to receive such a privileged private education. My mom always reminded us to work hard to be the best students so we could grow up to be useful to society. These memories remain with me.

Things changed in sixth grade, when we lived at home with our parents. A private chauffeur drove us to the same school, however, with an even tighter schedule.

When I was in high school, my normal day included Aikido in the morning from 6:00 a.m. to 7:30 a.m., then school from 8:00 a.m. until noon. Our chauffeur picked up my brother from his school, La Salle de Taberd, a famous all-boys' Catholic school, where he was taught by the La Salle Christian Brothers, before coming to pick up my three sisters and me to go home for lunch.

Depending on the day, we would then go to a private tutor for either math, chemistry, or physics between 1:30 p.m. and 3:30 p.m., and then return to school from 4:00 p.m. to 6 p.m. On Tuesday and Thursday, we went to the music conservatory from 6:30 p.m. to 8:30 p.m. to learn music solfège, theory, and history. We returned home for dinner and homework. On Saturday, we had private piano lessons, and Sunday was for church. I seldom went out to parties or social occasions. Instead, I spent most of my time studying and practicing piano.

I liked to use my wisdom collection book. This book contained a collection of proverbs based on philosophy, psychology, and personality. I didn't realize what personality was, but I was fascinated with analysis and interpretation of each facial and body trait. Someone with a round, full-shaped face was a kindhearted person, while someone with a bony face and a square jaw lacked loyalty. A hooked nose indicated wickedness, a beauty mark near the lips area depicted a sign of gluttony, etc. These weren't meant to be entirely accurate interpretations, but I was intrigued to know about them.

My life and needs seemed to be well taken care of with a chauffeur, two maids, my mother, and my father, who was the sole provider. Most of my life, I was an "open book." I was straightforward, honest, aggressive, impatient, and fast, but, at the same time, suspicious. I was told that I was an idealist with the mind of the fictional English spy James Bond. I used to dream of being an ambassador or a peacemaker when I grew up. Conservative, moral, and self-motivated, I wanted to be independent and a heroine. If I ever saw someone being picked on, beaten down, or less fortunate, I did what I could to help them. If that meant protecting them or speaking up for them, I'd do it. Without any hesitation, I accepted them as my friends.

~ ~ ~

Reflections

Have you had something bad turn out to be the best thing that could have happened to you?

I used to feel that I was neglected and punished because I lived with a strict private teacher. I missed home so much that I wondered at the time if my parents even loved me. What I didn't realize was that this foundation of routine and discipline set me up for future success and strength. It gave me the tools to strive and the momentum to achieve with structure and system.

I'm grateful to my parents for giving me this fortune, even if I didn't appreciate it at the time. By having this experience, I tend to give others, especially my children, chances to reconsider their judgments or opinions, knowing that time can make a difference. I know the process in coming to a decision is a matter of experiencing, understanding, affirming, and deciding. I learned to see the hidden positive benefits within negative situations. This gives me the inclination to acknowledge and lift up myself, and others, to a more fulfilled and joyful life.

Rose's Principle #2: Discipline

An army that enforces the right type of discipline upon its soldiers will achieve amazing results. This is also true for the average person.

Discipline is a requirement for success in every objective we set. Whether we're aiming for better fitness, higher education, a solid business or career, or anything else we want to achieve, we must have discipline to take us to the next level.

It is the foundation of success and must be started early with good habits that turn to routines and become natural to us.

This is one of the important requirements for any decent human being; it needs to be exercised with love from childhood on for the child to become a productive, constructive and decent citizen. Those children who are left neglected in front of the TV or who spend their time playing games or in idleness without a constructive and disciplined schedule can turn out to be troublemakers. These children become adults who refuse responsibility or refuse to obey rules and regulations.

It takes effort and great caring to raise our children with discipline. It is critical not only for the individual's sake, but for the building of community among well-behaved people.

Exercise Action Steps:

Whether you are still in school, in the work world, or a housewife or mother—in whatever stage you may be—set some schedules with discipline based on your goals for maximum productivity. We all have only 24 hours a day, no more and no less. It is up to us to organize a schedule with a focus in mind.

As for me, I always drink a big glass of water after waking up. I see that I exercise with a selected fitness video for one hour at least three times a week. Afterward, I make a complete smoothie, then get ready to work on my scheduled plan. So, no matter how busy I am, I make sure to have my one-hour intense exercise done, at least three times a week to maintain my fitness. I have never ceased working out, even during pregnancy. Discipline is the key to achieve what you want. Prioritize and focus.

3

Before the Fall of South Vietnam

When I was in middle school, I was very serious and uptight. My focus was on being a good girl and a good student, something others frequently misunderstood; they thought I was a snob. I was always busy with a very tight schedule and had no time to relax or fool around like other kids. On top of that, I was driven to be ahead in everything I did and was very much a loner. I was living on my own island without the need to be social; what I actually felt, however, was fear. I felt safer not associating with others.

It didn't help that, from kindergarten on, my classmates bullied me because of my Chinese heritage. They believed that I was somehow responsible for the thousand years of Chinese invasion and domination of Vietnam. The girls teased and mocked me. I was an easy target. Every dirty look or cold remark brought me to tears. Those little insignificant words and actions cut my soft, innocent heart and mind like sharp knives, so I tried to protect my inner vulnerability and sensitivity by pretending to be tough.

Then one day when I was in seventh grade, a very joyful Vietnamese nun returned from Hong Kong to teach our Bible class. Her outgoing, cheerful personality amazed me. Her cheerful laughter made me question my own serious and gloomy disposition.

Under the light of this nun's positive energy, I changed. The confident, happy Rose people know today awoke and flourished. I figured out that my cold, unfriendly outer shell was causing a lot of my problems. That outer shield of seriousness reflected my fear of being mistreated and my anger at being bullied. It didn't protect me, however, but actually caused more distance and misunderstanding. So, I metamorphosed into a new person. I smiled more, laughed more, and dared more. I let go of that shy, withdrawn child and moved into who I truly was.

What a difference from then on! I understood that, by trusting myself and my inner strength, I didn't need to appear tough. I no longer had to prove myself to anybody. This breakthrough allowed me to become a newly confident and joyous person with a different outlook of who I was or who I should be.

Starting from sixth grade, I was enrolled in a martial arts program called Aikido with Sensei Phong Thanh Dang. Three times a week, I went to the Tenshinkai School in the early morning. (*Tenshinkai* means "Organization of Heavenly Hearts.")

My teacher, Sensei Phong, was among the first generation of Aikido students in Vietnam to graduate with the rank of Shodan (1st Dan). In 1967, the Aikikai Aikido Headquarters officially recognized the Vietnam Aikido Association as one of its members. In 1999, Sensei Phong was inducted into the World Martial Arts Hall of Fame twice for his expertise in Aikido and for his lifetime of achievement and dedication to the martial arts. He was featured in *Black Belt* Magazine, the world's leading magazine of self-defense, in an article titled "Aikido's Entering Throw: Sweep Your Opponent off His Feet" with Irimi Nage and in another article entitled "The Grateful Art."

At first, I signed up to learn this martial art for protection from the bullies at school. However, it turned out to be more than just that. My teacher always asked me to speak up louder. My face would burn, my voice tremble like a lizard with a chopped-off tail. But with Aikido training, I became more in control of my nerves in situations that used to make me extremely nervous—playing the piano for annual exam by multiple piano professors at the National Music Conservatory of South Vietnam, reciting in front of the classroom, or any public presentation. The new training I had, however, helped me learn to tap into energies of all kinds, from deep breathing to meditating.

And it didn't just help me with my nerves; it gave me confidence and key techniques of mind, body, and soul balance I could apply in my daily life. I will always be grateful for my training in this "Grateful Art."

I wish to continue pursuing this unique art, as its wisdom has turned me into a person of self-control and courage. This has contributed greatly to my inner strength and the harmony of my own relationships through my life's journey.

~ ~ ~

Reflections

Do you let what others think, say, or do control your outlook on life? Do you laugh or smile frequently every day? Look in the mirror: You are who God says you are. Consciously smile with confidence and joy that you are blessed just by being alive and the person you are.

Laughter is excellent medicine for health and a youthful appearance. So laugh on, and be fully present every second of your life!

Rose's Principle #3: Be Positive in New Learning

Even though I was bullied, I had the opportunity to be educated and learn Aikido. A gentle kind of martial arts for self-defense purposes, it taught me self-control of mind, body, and soul balance. I realized it was more important to recognize the positive force of any negative situation instead of drowning myself in suffering. I refused to be the victim of bullying, and I chose a solution.

I found myself so appreciative of the opportunity to learn something new and different than what most Asian girls of the Eastern culture would have considered.

So, be open-minded when searching for solutions. Turn this into an opportunity to learn something new and different.

Exercise Action Steps:

Looking back at the differences between the two educational systems, European and the American, I see the pros and the cons in both. The European system makes you learn so many subjects, but there is a lack of the specialty aspect of American education. . It's good to focus on one thing at a time and become expert; however, it's also important to be well-rounded, so don't neglect to widen your horizon by being open-minded and always wanting to learn more.

When we were young, most of us did not know what our real talent or passion would be. So, we might have tried different things, such as sports, art, photography, literature, music, technology, acting, singing, fashion, martial arts, and the like. This is fine, while you're learning what you're best at. While you're doing it, pay attention and recognize your own passion or talent. Concentrate on one or two prominent talents and become as expert in them as possible.

Also, be realistic about what the result of your chosen path could be. This will help you as you wisely work toward greater success. I did not have this wisdom when I came to a new country, embraced a new culture, and tried to get along in a new system. I just decided to go to college and continue with piano, while my English was barely usable. How did I move forward? By striving to catch up and make it.

4

Beauty in a War-Torn Country

Since North and South Vietnam were at war, for security and safety reasons, we didn't visit too many places outside of the city except for a few memorable locations such as Vung Tàu. Vũng Tàu was the port capital of Bà Ria-Vũng Tàu Province, located on a peninsula in southern Vietnam. Once a French colonial town, it's now a popular seaside resort that draws visitors from Ho Chi Minh City, who arrive by hydrofoil. Its long, busy stretch of beach has verdant mountains as a backdrop.

Every summer, we vacationed for a week in a beachfront villa with lots of fruit trees in the garden. We could walk straight onto the beach from our rooms. We used to get up early before the tide rose high on the rocks to catch the clams and the crabs. Our great-grandmother would cook the clams we caught with fish sauce and lots of black pepper to be eaten with Jasmine rice. That was such a simple but delicious dish that I still vividly remember—and sometimes crave!

Then my father would drive us to another part of the sandy beach where we could swim all day. We had plenty of seafood, such as steamed crabs, clams, and shrimp, and Tamarind soup with fresh fish or crispy calamari.with fresh vegetables and rice for lunch and dinner.

Another unforgettable place was called Đà Lat The capital of Lâm Đong Province, in southern Vietnam's Central Highlands, it was centered on a lake and golf course. Surrounded by hills, pine forests, lakes, and waterfalls, it was known as the "City of Eternal Spring" for its temperate climate and was developed as a resort by the French in the early 1900s. Many reminders of its colonial heritage remain.

Đà Lat was one of my favorite vacation places because of the cool weather and the high mountains. It was the rare paradise in a hot and humid country.

One night while I was there visiting this simple and humble countryside, it was bombed. I held my breath. My maid was more nervous for my safety than I was, because she knew what was really going on. I didn't understand how dangerous it was at the time, but that experience has stayed with me. I still wonder how those people could live in fear every day and night and realize how blessed I was to be a city girl.

~ ~ ~

Reflections

Living in a country at war, it was a luxury for me to be able to travel anywhere. I was able to experience only a few places, but each place had its own character and landmarks that created special memories and learning experiences for me and my family.

Bonds that come about naturally when a family spends time together are priceless in anyone's childhood. The memories that remain when I think of the good old times together with my energetic father, sweet old great-grandmother, gentle mother, and my innocent brother and sisters are so precious in my heart. I learned that traveling to a new place enriches my life immeasurably. It allows me to decompress and rejuvenate my spirit, regardless of the circumstances.

Rose's Principle #4: Find Joy in Traveling

It is a joy to be able to travel, to discover new opportunities, learn new lessons, and appreciate what you have. Traditionally, a woman's role was that of housewife, a cook, and in-house person. This is no longer the case.

You can travel around the world, so don't limit yourself to what is only within your comfort zone. Instead, stretch your plans to include new places, new cultures, new challenges, new food, and new customs. These will enrich you intellectually and spiritually. The more experiences one has through traveling, the more open-minded and flexible one can become to appreciate the bad, the good, and the best.

Through travel, I discovered more of who I was, what I liked or disliked, how to make certain adjustments wisely, and how to make things better for myself and humanity. This appreciation can inspire one to grow and, in turn, inspire others to open their minds to other points of view and cultures. Most of all, travel can make you feel both humble and excited: there's so much more to see and learn than any of us realizes in our comfort zone. The more we see, the more we know how much we don't know.

Exercise Action Steps:

Remember to write an entry into your journal about each travel experience you have. If you did not do that on past trips, do it now, either on your iPad, phone, or notepad. Make notes of the time, places, experiences, and feelings you have. Organize the pictures with dates and locations.

Spiritual journaling in nature offers a break from our hectic, overscheduled lives by providing space and time to breathe, center ourselves, and play in the woods by ourselves and with others—human and non-human! Keep a nature journal and explore how journaling in nature helps us to be centered, mindful, and attentive to our own spirits, as well as those of other creatures.

Share this practice with your children, too; encourage them to write in a journal every day about their daily highlights or memories, whether they go on a trip or not. Making this a daily discipline can be rewarding in more ways than one, as it gives them a way to capture the memories that make life special.

5

Self-Image and Self-Help

*B*ecause I attended a private Catholic girls' school from kindergarten until the fall of Saigon, I spent a good portion of my childhood in uniforms. These uniforms didn't allow for creativity or self-expression. Every school day, I had to wear the same style of white shirt and blue, pleated skirt. As a result, I *felt* boring; I looked like everyone else. There was no individuality, just another cog in the wheel. This desire to express myself came to a head in the sixth grade when I discovered fashion and style, and that I could show people who I was through my clothes.

So, I started designing my own clothes. I was passionate about choosing the right materials and colors for each outfit. I mixed and matched styles and colors and created my own custom-made outfits. Every outfit was an original work of art in my eyes. Every time I didn't have to wear my school uniform, I wore the clothes I designed. My classmates and friends always commented on my artistic creativity. This is when I learned a valuable lesson: that I never had to go for "brands" but for "styles" instead.

Only when many people had complimented me on my style did I give myself credit for talent in this area.

I admit that I was lucky. I had a family who could afford for me to do this. They gave me a wonderful foundation, but I didn't appreciate how much I had until April 30, 1975, when the communists took over South Vietnam. On that day, when the city was in chaos with people running wild in the streets and young guys with guns were yelling, "Victory," all my hard work and studies seemed to be in vain.

As it turned out, I was unable to pursue this passion until we escaped to the States. Once here, in this great country, my talent served me well, especially in those first years when we struggled to make ends meet. Even with little money, I honored that creative self and dressed myself like a queen, as the work of art each of us is. No one knew I was on a budget.

It's amazing what the right clothes can do for a person and his or her self-confidence. I know what it has done for me and for the women who've asked me to help them transform themselves from being "ugly ducklings" to the beautiful, confident women they've always been. They just needed the right clothes to see their beauty. When you can see your own beauty, you can find self-love.

Later in life, my spouse has often complimented me, saying I have a gifted artistic eye for elegance. For me, it's fun and enjoyable to make myself, as well as other women and men, look their best. And it seems natural to me, something I truly appreciate.

I have been told many times that I should share my expertise, but I've decided I need to focus on other, more important, missions — though it would be just so much fun to work with people who appreciate beauty and art and boost their own confidence and joy. To be able to love material things, to clothe them with tender grace, and yet not be attached to them, is a great service.

God expects us to make this world our own, and not loll around in it as though it were a rented tenement. We can only make it our own through some service, and that service is to lend it love and beauty from our soul.

You already know the difference between the beautiful, the tender, the hospitable, and the mechanically neat and monotonously useful. Gross utility kills beauty. All over the world, we have mammoth organizations with immense production and output, but often they obstruct the path to real life. Civilization is waiting for a great consummation, for an expression of its soul in beauty. This must be your contribution to the world.

~ ~ ~

Reflections:

Since most of my school year was spent in a uniform with a white shirt and a blue, pleated skirt, I struggled to express who I was.

Fortunately, I had the luxury to have tailor-made clothes. Creating my own elegant style at such a young age was exhilarating to me. Not to boast, but this artistic bent helped me confirm the recognition of how the beauty of color and textiles can enhance a person's image. I don't take this gift for granted. I am so grateful that I had the chance to develop this art; it has been an asset all my life.

Over the years, this art became just an example of learning to know who I really was, not just mentally, psychologically, spiritually, and intellectually, but also physically. Knowing and admitting my own "flaws" or shortcomings — literally, in that I was very petite! — is itself an art. It helps us know and show the best parts of ourselves without making fools of ourselves in ignorance.

This connection between recognizing physical limitations or disabilities and appreciating gifts has a lot to do with the desire to be a better person. Acknowledging shortcomings, ironically enough, enables us to also accept our own beauty. Refusing to do so is like when we accept the beauty of roses, but forget reality of their thorns.

Learning to express yourself and honoring who you are is loving yourself. Loving yourself honors God and shows Him how grateful we are for the gifts He has given us. This applies to every bit of the care we give ourselves.

Rose's Principle #5: Image

Each person has only one body. To feel confident and energetic, one must dress with style and elegance. To be elegant and have style, one must try to stay fit and healthy.

Whether you are married or single, it's important to continue to take care of yourself, physically and mentally, in a loving way. How you treat yourself will affect your overall image, inside and out. Part of keeping a relationship fresh and loving, too, is being able to love yourself enough to keep yourself fit and healthy.

With this simple principle of respecting and loving oneself, I've helped many couples rekindle their relationships. It shows when we care. It is a conscious effort to improve our outward body confidence to feel positive about our own body. It works wonders on our self-esteem and that of everyone around us, especially our children. We can build confidence by being kinder to ourselves, accepting our pros and cons, and making realistic improvements.

Even though inner beauty is an important factor for complete and lasting happiness, beauty and image can influence your life in different ways. How you look shows how strong-willed a person you are, because it takes great effort and discipline to make yourself stay fit and energetic. There is a price for everything. Hard, firm muscles are built from hard work, and how much one cares about being healthy reflects how strong one's mind has to be to achieve the result. In the end, it is self-control and self-love, because unless you really know how to truly love yourself, it is hard to know how to love others.

Exercise Action Steps:

Be kind to yourself: Purposefully smile at yourself in the mirror and find at least one thing every day that you like about yourself and how you look.

Get positive: Start saying positive things about your body and your personality out loud. The more you say these things, the more likely you are to believe them.

Write yourself a letter: Write positive messages about how you look and how you'd like to feel on sticky notes and stick them all around your house. Messages like "Hello, Gorgeous" or "What's cooking, good looking?" or "You are perfect just the way you are" are great reminders for both you and your children.

Learn your solutions: Wear high heels if you think you want to look taller, wear light and loose material to create a thinner illusion, cover up the not-so-attractive parts, and reveal the confident parts. Most of all, accept your flaws and make some realistic improvements in natural ways and enhance your highlights with confidence. With the right attitude, there is always a possibility for improvement.

6

Life after the Communist Takeover

*I*n 1975, at 16 years old, I began a new chapter in my life. No more school, no more music, no more martial arts, no more private classes, no more maid or chauffeur. Many wealthy people committed suicide. When families were forced to honor Ho Chi Minh, the party leader, above all else, even their parents, many families were broken apart. Children were taught to turn against anyone who didn't comply with what the communist regime dictated. Day in and day out, people were constantly brainwashed with banners and songs, by all levels of media, from the time they were in preschool.

Ears and eyes monitored every sermon from the churches. Group gatherings were guarded under strict rules and regulations and needed a permit. The wealthy lived in constant fear, not knowing when it'd be their turn to be taken away for no reason. The more assets and properties one owned, the more likely they were to be labeled a "blood sucker" by the communists' policy.

Later, I found out my father was one of the lucky men who wasn't turned in to the new leaders by poor people. Without knowing, he'd helped a lot of the poor before the fall of the previous regime. Many of them happened to be undercover communists. Luckily, my father was just a very generous and kind man. This made a big impression on me, and it taught me that doing good deeds can at times bring you protection from unexpected dangers.

There was fear of reprisal among remaining businessmen, Catholics, and those allied with the U.S. The new communist soldiers could come to your house and claim any asset as common property and take it away at any time. They came to our house and took our cars, our TV, our motorcycles, and more. My father let them have anything without resistance. It was more important to have our lives than our assets. At least, after they confiscated what they wanted, they left us alone for a bit.

Teachers and government officials were taken to a re-education camp; therefore, I quit school when it devolved into a propaganda tool.

My father had worked too hard to give up his business, but knew his family needed to get out. One day, my brother's violin teacher came to the house and delivered a warning to my mom. His experience with communism when he escaped from North Vietnam in 1954 had taught him how dangerous this situation was. He advised my mom to do everything she could to get us out of there. But how were we going to escape?

My father's first attempt was to arrange marriages in France for me and my younger sister, paying a French woman plenty for passports that were never produced, before backing out because of worry for his daughters' safety.

Guard towers had been placed inside the city and out to monitor suspicious activity, but my father spent hours observing shift changes and memorizing watch patterns, hatching an escape plan with a friend to secure a boat and float the family away.

One day, my father told my mother to give him all the jewelry and gold that she had. The day before we were to leave, he took everything she gave him down to a boat. However, the people who were supposed to be helping us tricked him and took everything instead.

I didn't know many of the details, but one night, he was taken away with no warning or reason. This frightened us. We had no idea where he was and when, or if, he'd ever return. My mom managed to bribe someone to find him. It turned out one of his escape organizers or the boat owner had sold him out. They tortured him with electric shocks and beat him, making him write a daily confession report of his crime, planning to escape.

In the end, my father's business skills saved him. He found a way to negotiate a settlement wherein he would write a report claiming a lesser amount of the actual gold stolen in exchange for his release via a public trial. This trial was conducted by some poor, uneducated city monitors in the open street of the town. The bottom line was that my father couldn't reclaim the confiscated gold, allowing the bad guys to keep it and split it among themselves.

My father and family were never more humiliated, but my father was willing to pay the price. He was released under the condition that he had to physically report to the town's guard every day.

This only strengthened his determination to get us out. He sent us outside and told us to get a tan by swimming among the fishermen; there, we were able to keep our ears open for any avenue of escape. Ironically enough, during this period of my life, I had more free time and new friends than ever before.

~ ~ ~

Reflections

I remember great disappointment and fear of the unknown when South Vietnam fell into the hands of the communists. For a time I couldn't help regretting having studied so hard and missing out on all the fun that most other teenagers might have enjoyed, such as going to parties and dancing. I truly felt like that was the end of my world.

Internal pain can capture our attention and hold it hostage. Many of us lead "lives of quiet desperation," as Thoreau once said. The greater part of our energy is siphoned off by fears, angers, guilt, hatred, loneliness, and frustrations. We can find ourselves with little zest and even less strength to join the dance of life or sing its songs. We can feel like tightrope walkers trying to keep our balance, afraid of the stress that can flip them into an emotional or mental abyss.

As social stresses increase, the quiet desperation can flare up into acute and painful symptoms. A man loses his job and develops bleeding ulcers. A mother whose child dies goes into severe, prolonged depression. The protracted stress of the Vietnam War left much of the American psyche strained and sour.

So many sources of stress make contemporary life a precarious adventure. Many people are willing to settle for survival and safety. However, the fear of the unknown made me restless to find a way out by unlocking my closed world.

I believed that when one door was closed, other doors would be opened. So, thank God for the desperation: it led me to a new world, one that exceeded my expectations.

Rose's Principle #6: Persistence

Even though my father failed in his first attempt to organize an escape, he persisted in trying again. Torture and prison didn't stop him. He continued until he found another way to lead us to freedom.

Keep trying until you find a way. This is one of the principles that has helped me to achieve my goals. When I set goals with conviction and determination, I can accomplish anything, regardless of the obstacles. All change in the quality of life must grow out of a change in one's vision of reality. There can be no real and permanent change unless this vision changes. Open your eyes to find new light to a new way, no matter what or how long it will take. Know your purpose to thrive to achieve.

As a daughter, I was being obedient and followed my parents' guidance and direction. However, I also wished for nothing less than the best in life — at least the degree of comfort I had before the Communists took over, certainly nothing less. I set my standard and learned to find a solution for a better result. I was not willing to surrender to fate or circumstance.

Exercise Action Steps:

When you are stuck with something or experience a crisis or challenge, pause to reassess or reevaluate the facts, conditions, and circumstances.

1. Check out the people involved.

2. Identify possible causes, including timing, people, location, and motives.

3. Look for new blood, new resources, or connections to create a different vision.

4. Come up with creative strategies, using other people's resources to achieve objectives.

5. Have the courage to admit your own limitations and ask for help.

7

The Quest for Freedom

I n 1976, a year after my father's trial, we were continuing to keep a low profile. Our goal to escape to freedom remained. My father realized his next arrest could be his last, but he again plotted an escape. Despite having lost everything in the first attempt, he somehow managed to find some rich sponsors. They trusted him completely to arrange for another boat escape for them. Because he was putting the escape together and taking the risk of being caught, we were included in the bargain.

I still marvel at how he arranged this. With the fire of hope for a better tomorrow, we never stopped praying for a solution, a way out, a new light for freedom.

One day, during a heavy rain storm, my cousin, two young friends, great-grandmother, all five of my sisters and brother, including myself, and my mom left in a well-covered van driven by my father to somewhere by the river of Bien-Hoa.

In complete silence, we arrived at a secret hideout in the evening. There was no moon on the night of June 1, 1976. It was so intense and mysterious in this place where we met many other people who had been hiding and waiting for us. Not too long after, people loaded onto two small sampan boats. All wearing black, we were told to lie flat against the wooden planks. From there, we moved to some small row boats that awaited on a very narrow stream. My father carried my hunch-backed great-grandmother, who was in her eighties, and put her in the tiny wooden rowboat, where we y down as close as sardines in a can. Holding our breath, we obeyed my father's whispered signals. At the time, I wasn't sure how many rowboats traveled through this narrow stream to a river, then out to a wider canal, where we were transferred to two wooden boats about 25 feet long. Later, I learned about 94 people were involved in this escape, most of them women. Besides my great-grandmother, there was another older woman in her nineties and a one-week-old baby who was kept silent with sleeping pills.

Our two wooden boats were supposed to meet a larger and better-equipped boat with provisions, which would take us to Hong Kong and the beginning of our long oceanic journey, but it didn't show up.

We waited impatiently at the Canal Cap St. Jacques for a short while, but nothing happened. Realizing another arrest would mean certain death, my father ordered the boats to push on into the open sea. Our "provisions" at that point were a few cans of condensed milk, and some water. We were in no way prepared for an open sea trip to Hong Kong.

Before we went further, we sank the small rowboats out of sight. Then, we rushed out to sea as fast as we could. On our boat in the ocean, I took charge as an inner captain, while my father was the external leader in charge of the navigation and looking out for any sign of danger.

Inside my boat were about 50 of us. Some of the people who funded the trip were acting privileged, superior, and selfish; I refused to tolerate that, especially when our engine area had a leak and we all had to bail out the excess water to prevent the boat from sinking. When a couple of these arrogant folks refused to pitch in, I ordered them to work along with the rest of us. I wasn't gentle about it, either!

Our two wooden boats operated well for three days, but soon we ran out food and water. Large sea creatures—dolphins or sharks—circled the boats, which were tethered together to save gasoline.

I looked at the vast expanse of ocean. Surrounded by water that no one could drink, it was torture. Throats parched, we were growing listless and discouraged. Without water, we would die. Desperation was setting in. The thought of a drop of water at that moment was indescribable.

Thanks to that experience, I will never forget how precious drinking water can be. Cries and wails could be heard above the crashing and heaving sea. We were so desperate for water! Then, suddenly, a large storm hit and engulfed us. The rope was cut to prevent the boats from smashing into each other.

Was this storm a miracle? A gift from God? It didn't matter: I sprang into action. While everyone else hid inside the cabin, I sat in the open area of one end of the boat and tried to catch as much water as I could with any container I had. I clung to the rim of the boat as waves large enough to swallow our boat in one gulp crashed around us. How I survived that storm, I'll never know. I might have used my Aikido *qi*, my super power strength, to resist being thrown off into the ocean. To me, it was a miracle.

The preciousness of drinking water and how we were saved in the nick of time will stay with me for the rest of my life.

We traveled on for another couple of days, I believe. Then we ran out of gasoline. Floating aimlessly, we hoped someone would rescue us. Hours passed in silence… except for the sound of the waves. They were like an invincible force that made you feel helpless and small; in other words, you could feel how almighty the Creator was. All this time, we looked to the horizon, hoping to see some land and praying for a rescuer.

On our fifth day on the boat, the hungry, thirsty, exhausted groups saw a large fishing vessel in the distance and headed toward us. Before we could get their attention, though, a huge patrol ship also powered into sight and shot its guns into the air.

We had our arms up, wondering what would happen. Who could they be? Only when the boats pulled alongside did we see the communist flag painted on the side. It turned out to be a Vietnamese communist patrol ship. Fear consumed us. All the work and hardship was apparently futile.

"Where are you going?" the captain shouted. There was no answer.

He asked again.

Finally, my father said, "To search for freedom."

"Freedom?" the captain replied. "You've made a big mistake."

My father volunteered to go on their ship to talk, while we raised our voices in prayers, our arms still up. We'd gotten so far. Would we have to go back? How could that be? What was going to happen to us? I believed my father, as the leader, would be executed. We'd be sent to a concentration labor camp and our families would be torn apart.

I couldn't imagine how I could accept living in such conditions. It wasn't the terror of losing my life, but the terror of losing my family that began to overcome my fear. . Gradually, I felt my numbness and terror become something else entirely: a determination to do something.

The passengers were loaded onto the vessel, where we were thankful to be given rice and tea. But another round of anguish was audible when the captain ordered the boat to return to Saigon.

They ordered us to get on the patrol ship, one by one, and grouped us in a corner of it. If you were in this situation, what would you do? Being just a young girl, feeling like a small sparrow on a huge ship, I decided to walk through the ship, from one end to the other. For some reason, no one stopped me. Was I afraid? I vividly remember how strongly my mind refused to accept the consequences of being taken back to hell. I just knew that it was the rose of freedom that I wanted and that the phoenix had to rise out of this situation. Could it be the Holy Spirit who blinded the guards to my presence, or did they underestimate me because they assumed a weakness of the female gender? I think it was because I was just like a cute, little bird, harmless in the eyes of these male soldiers and the guns they had on board. (Specifically, the crew had two rifles and a portable anti-tank weapon.)

At the opposite end of the ship in the back, a soldier was holding his gun while standing at his post. I started chatting with him. After he found out that the man who came up alone was my father, he talked to me. He shared that their leader was called Chu Ba (Uncle Three). The soldier had seen my father on his knees, pleading and begging and offering himself and all the gold we had on our boats in exchange for the freedom of the rest of our party. The communist leader wouldn't cut a deal because he wanted credit for everything, the gold *and* the people. But the soldier was touched by my father's begging and bravery because he was a soldier in the former South Vietnamese military. During our chat, I learned that there were thirteen soldiers on board, some huge muscular men with guns, and a cannon in the middle of the ship, down below deck.

Everyone was ordered inside the cabin of the ship, except me. On top of the cabin, two soldiers stood guard. My mom gave them coffee she'd mixed with valium.

My father already knew who the captain was. Whispering, I shared with my father the information I'd learned about the men, their guns, and positions. My father and I didn't have to say much to each other, but it seemed like we were on the same wavelength and fueled with the same determination. The energy of King Win and me, his sparrow, was very intensely aligned.

Accordingly, to Dr. Wayne Dyer, energy in the air can be transferred and connected between people, and it certainly seemed true in that moment. We seemed to read each other's minds as we focused on escape or revolt. We were going to do something … somehow. This is what my father said, whispering to my mother in Chinese:

"We've decided to fight back," he began. "We have a fifty-fifty chance of survival. If we win, we live. If we don't, we're dead. But it's better than doing nothing. If we fail, at least we'll die quickly, instead of by torture."

The plan was to attack each crew member simultaneously and wrestle the weapons away. My mother and father then synchronized their watches.

Two guards with guns ordered some of our people onto one of our two boats, which were being towed behind the ship, to bail out the water leaking inside the engine cabin. Two others went down to the other boat to retrieve our gold. They pointed randomly at any male figures, among them my brother and my cousin. Knowing that my father had planned a takeover, I stopped the soldiers from taking my only brother and cousin to our boats. I really don't know what kind of authority or power I had, but I did it. I just pulled my brother and cousin over to my side, refusing to let them go. For some reason, our captors didn't object. Instead, a couple of the cowards from our group volunteered to go.

With four guards on the other boats, nine guards were left on board: two guards at one end, two on the top deck who might have fallen asleep from the valium, three underneath the engine chamber, including the captain, and two in the back, including the one who talked to me.

I'm not sure how my father communicated with the others to coordinate the revolt, but, suddenly, my father and another man rushed the guy I was talking to, catching him by surprise in an arm wrestle. My father found the barrel of the rifle pointed at his stomach as he grappled for control of the rifle, hands grasped tightly near the trigger. During those split seconds, he—an avowed atheist—vowed instead to turn to God! At 2 a.m., with the lights of Vietnam visible from the deck, gunshots rang out.

I jumped into the cabin.

Gunshots echoed from below, and a huge guy raced through the cabin in a panic. I pushed the old lady out of his way. Had I not and the guard had grabbed one of us as a hostage, it would've changed everything. I'm not sure how it would've turned out.

I'm not sure how long the revolt lasted, but it seemed no longer than a lightning strike. The man fighting my father had his gun pressed into my father, but, miraculously, he pulled it up and didn't shoot my dad. My father's palms were blistered during the fight for the rifle, but he was otherwise unhurt, and now he was a believer.

Before long, we controlled the ship, though a few of us were injured. A bullet grazed the eyebrow of my third sister, a boy was shot through the leg, blowing his calf open, and a girl also was hit under her breast. One of our men was pushed into the ocean during the initial confrontation. But the mutiny was successful.

The two asleep on the deck happened to be soldiers of the former regime, and the captain survived and followed us thereafter. Those who died in the confrontation were thrown into the ocean.

With the ship secured, we turned to the wounded. We had little in the way of supplies and had to make do with what was on hand. We used a tobacco bag that happened to be laying around to cover open wounds and control bleeding. One of our people was a nurse, who helped tend to the injuries, wrapping the wounds with cloth diapers. Thank God, she was with us.

We continued to sail toward freedom for the next two nights, but the wounded were losing a lot of blood. They'd grown pale and had the purple cast to their skin you see on cadavers. Worry that their wounds would become infected and they'd die haunted us. Only by the grace of God did we meet a Thai fishing boat.

Because a communist flag was painted on the wall in the middle of our cabin, it took some convincing to get them to believe we weren't communists, but once we managed to do so, they guided us to the border between Thailand and Malaysia, a province called Narathiwat. Our ship anchored on the southeastern coast there. But the locals, unsure what to think about a communist vessel in their midst, did not allow us refugees to disembark.

They didn't plan on us refusing to leave. But my dad made it clear they shoot all of us if they wanted. We didn't care anymore. We simply were not going anywhere.

As we came into port and waited aboard the ship, the native people stared warily at us from the shore, their suspicion warring with curiosity. My father spoke Chinese in their dialect and asked for help for the wounded. The Thai contacted some American journalists, who came to our ship to conduct interviews. They then arranged for our wounded to be sent to the hospital.

A kind Thai man took me and my sister to town to shop for some clothes and fed us. In fact, if we continued on to Hong Kong, he was hoping to follow our ship to get out of Thailand. Instead, three CBS newsmen, Peter Collins, Richard Wagner, and Derek P. Williams, came to interview us.

How do I still remember their names after 39 years? I happened to find the business cards they gave me that day. Today, their business cards are valuable proof of my escape and survival. During the

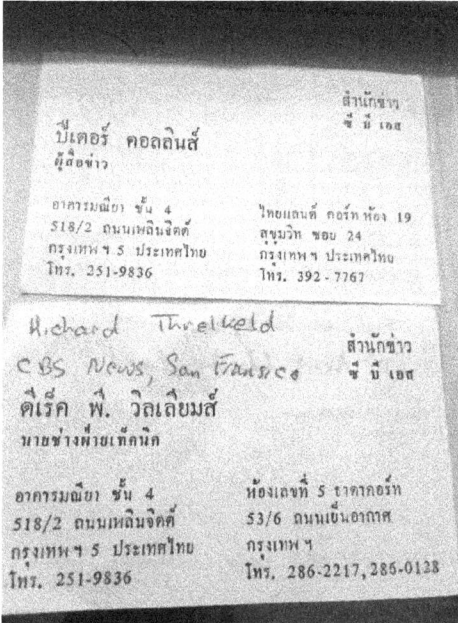

Business cards from the kind CBS reporters

interview, I refused to disclose the location of our escape from Vietnam. I wanted future escapees to have a chance, like we had.

Later, these three CBS journalists got on our ship and guided us to a refugee camp in Songkhla, where we lived for about two months before leaving for California. This was where I decompressed, and the fear that had shadowed me every day since the fall of Saigon started to fade away. When I looked at the ocean with my feet on the soil of Thailand, I wondered how I had survived all of what had just happened. That was when I realized that I could feel fear—but that it didn't control my destiny.

During our stay in the refugee camp, we slept on wooden beds that were surrounded by nets. The refugee camp wasn't comfortable at all. We showered in a portable standing box that was open on top—somewhat embarrassing, but nevertheless welcome in the heat. Despite the primitive living conditions there, though, we were grateful to be alive. We shared the fish from the patrol ship with the whole refugee camp. The abundance of fish reminded me of the miracle of two loaves of bread and fish that Jesus used to feed thousands of people. We rejoiced and were hopeful, even though we didn't know what would happen next. The extreme opposite conditions between rich and poor we'd experienced had left us all very aware of how volatile and fragile social status can be.

I was grateful that we were all finally safe. Out of 94 people, 91 of us remained alive, with only three wounded. Our story of escape and survival made headlines everywhere.

The CBS reporters contacted my aunt in California, and we were sponsored to leave Thailand close to two months thereafter, faster than most of the refugees there and more fortunate than many refugees in the later years who repatriated or died at sea— or in the camp—before they could resettle anywhere.

~ ~ ~

Reflections

What should you do if you were facing danger and death?

Facing Death Experience Formula

According to Gallup Polls, five percent of American adults have had near-death experiences. .

After days at sea, escaping communist Vietnam, and surviving a huge storm, our boat ran out of gasoline and was captured by a communist patrol ship that was armed with guns. We all thought we were going to die and would have if we hadn't avoided these three key mistakes:

3 Mistakes to Avoid if You Are Facing Death

Mistake #1: Panic

Mistake #2: No Plan

Mistake #3: No Action

I call mistake #1 the Jodie Foster mistake. Jodie Foster starred in the movie *The Panic Room*. She went into a room that wasn't in full working condition and ended up stuck there. While all ends well in this movie, that's not usually the case in real life. If you panic when facing death, you're more likely to die than if you stay calm.

Mistake #2 is what I refer to as the Tom Cruise mistake because it's the exact opposite of what he does in the *Mission Impossible* movies. His character always has a plan he carries out in a timely manner, one that saves his life. With a plan, you can survive.

The last mistake is what I refer to as the Jet Lee, or Arnold Schwarzenegger, mistake. These two men play action heroes. They will take action in order to survive any situation. If you are facing death and fail to take action, you may as well dig your own grave.

By staying calm, having a plan, and taking action, you have a better chance of surviving.

Rose Phan's CALM Formula to Survive Deadly Experiences:

1. **C**ontrol your breathing/Courage

2. **A**ct wisely and with a plan

3. **L**ead positively

4. **M**indset/Mastery of Fear (either accept death or take action with your plan). Your mindset can determine whether you live or die.

You can apply this formula in business, school, relationships, and life in general. Apply this when you are facing a crisis, conflict, or challenges. The most important (and simple) act you must take is to **control your breathing**.

This action is crucial to get control of your nerves and prevent any irrational action . By using the basic technique of "Qigong," energy breathing for the control of the mind and body, you can bring harmony and balance back into your being. This will calm you, allowing you to think clearly. It seems simple and basic, but it is the key to self-control.

Take a deep breath, inhale to below your belly button and hold it, then release. Do this until your nerves are calm. Your body is smart, and it knows exactly how you're feeling. Even though sometimes you can try to ignore those feelings, if you don't calm yourself, the feelings will take over.

We most appreciate what we have when we lose it or almost lose it. Life is most precious at these times.

Rose's Principle # 7: Courage Over Fear!

Even though we were captured and in the hands of the communists, I didn't let fear overpower my will to survive. I refused to give up after everything I'd gone through to get there. I wasn't going to just sit there and let my family be taken back to Vietnam, where we could be put to death. Instead of accepting the situation and giving up, I walked in faith and believed I'd find a way for us to escape.

When our boat had a leak in the engine area, I delegated people to take turns pouring the water out so we did not sink. Knowing that a small hole could sink our boat is a lesson that I've applied in life, marriage, business, and friendship. I seem to have a knack for catching little details and facts that enable me to read people's minds and feelings, whether they are friends or foes. It takes effort and energy to care, pay attention, communicate, clarify, resolve, and make changes. It is the heart of caring that makes the difference. In the face of the strain of tasks beyond our strength, we must turn inward to the Source of strength. If we measure our human strength against the work we see immediately ahead, we'll feel hopeless. If we tackle it in that strength, we'll be frustrated.

There is no healthier lesson we can learn than our own limitations, provided this is accompanied by the resignation of our own strength and reliance on the strength of God. The wheel of life will fly apart unless it is spoked to the center; we'll merely go rushing onward without taking time to turn inward.

That drive to keep trying and not give up helped save our lives. It's the same drive that has brought me great success in all areas of my life.

So, never give up. Where there's a will, there's a way.

Exercise Action Steps:

1. Have a strong conviction and believe in it and yourself wholeheartedly.

2. Repeat a mantra, such as, "I know I can do it," "I am not afraid, for God is with me," or "No guts, no glory."

3. Strategize and follow your plan.

4. Listen to inputs from reliable and trusted sources, but don't let them influence you negatively.

5. Make your decision and take full responsibility without regret. Care enough to dare.

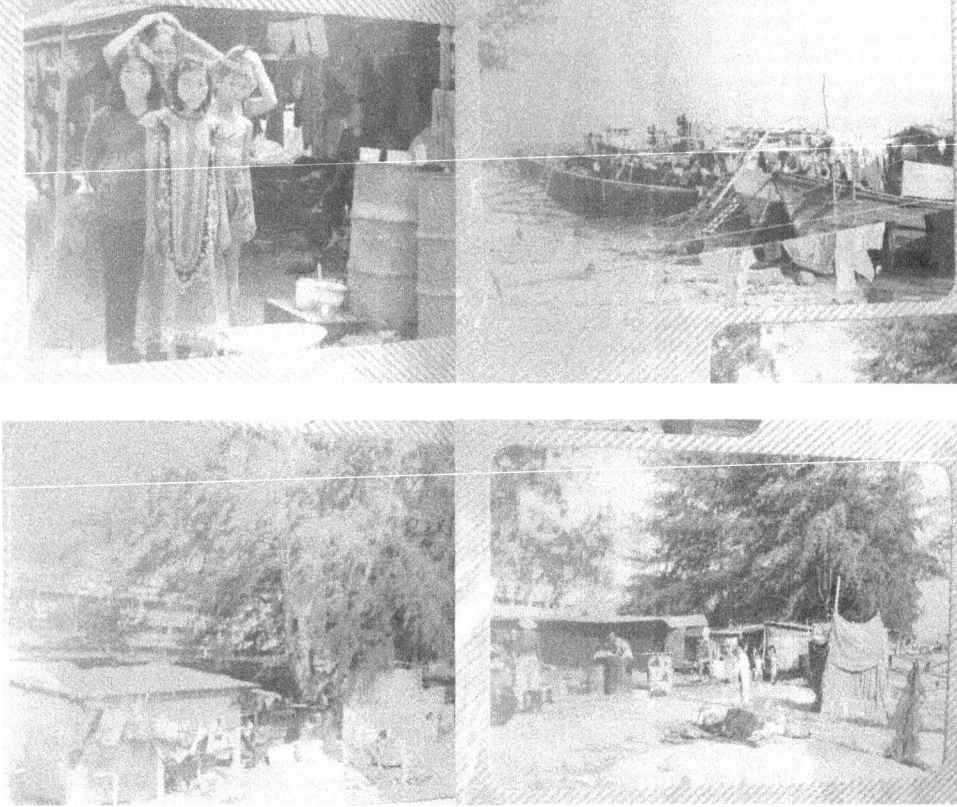

Pictures from my stay at the refugee camp

8

Life at Refugee Camp

D uring our stay in the refugee camp from June 8, 1976 to August 1, 1976, we slept on wooden beds surrounded by nets. One of scariest incidents I experienced was when the Thai guards at the camp expressed interest in me because I had light skin, and tried to show favor to me. They even attempted to sneak into our bed, but since we all slept on the same wooden bed, a loud scream scared them away. From then on, my parents were more cautious and let the girls sleep in the middle of the bed. We all became more alert and on guard due to that unexpected incident.

However, one day, my family got to sneak out of the camp with one of the guys who seemed to know the outside roads. Like tourists, we went to the beach and enjoyed Thai food. I honestly don't know how my father managed that special treat for our family and didn't ask. I was just so happy that we had such a good time for at least that one afternoon. The guard could have been bribed, but how and by whom, I am not sure. Another refugee came with us and brought his camera, which was how we took the pictures here.

Under the circumstances, we were very lucky to get away for one afternoon. Was that another blessing from the grace of God? Rarely were refugees allowed to enjoy any leisure time or luxuries. However, it happened to me and my family. Amazing, right?

Do you believe now that anything is possible, regardless of the circumstance? Treasure it and be thankful. I did and never forgot meeting two European couples at the beach, tourists who were French and Swiss. We spoke in French with these couples, who showed sympathy for our situation and became friends. After hearing our story, they loaned us their bikinis so we could swim. We even had our pictures taken with them. Looking at those pictures today, it is hard to believe that we were boat refugees in that picture. We just looked like Asian tourists on a beach in Thailand.

I lost contact with the French couple after that, but corresponded and kept in touch with the couple from Switzerland. He was a violinist in the World Orchestra (Orchestre du Monde from Switzerland), and his wife was a flutist. They were such a sweet couple. Later, I went to visit them in Geneva a couple of times, and they came to visit me in California once.

I experienced a broad range of experiences at the camp. Being there gave me plenty of time to contemplate of all them in silence.

Concentration in silence without effort is a state of perfect calm, accompanied by complete relaxation of the nerves and muscles of the body. You could say that the entire being becomes like the surface of calm water, reflecting the immense presence of the starry sky and its indescribable harmony.

And the waters are deep, so deep! And the silence grows, ever increasing...what silence! One wave of silence followed by another wave of more profound silence, then again, a wave of still more profound silence.

Have you ever *drunk silence*? If so, you know what meditation without effort is.

Despite the primitive living conditions in the refugee camp, we were so grateful to be alive. We rejoiced and were hopeful, even though we didn't know what would happen next. Many people had been there for a long time before we got there and were still there when we left.

Notice that the more you become a connoisseur of gratitude, the less you are the victim of resentment, depression, and despair. Gratitude acts as an elixir that gradually dissolves the hard shell of your ego—your need to possess and control—and transforms you into a generous being. The sense of gratitude produces true spiritual alchemy, making us magnanimous—large-souled.

Everyone's background and history was screened very carefully by the American government before their entrance into the USA was accepted. With the sponsorship of our aunt, who was a US citizen at the time, we were more fortunate than many to have our residency in California accepted so fast.

Believe it or not, a fortuneteller even read my mom's cards before our escape and told her I would become famous and wealthy later. Ha! I did not pay attention to such superstition.

~ ~ ~

Reflections

After the crisis in the ocean and arriving in Thailand, I had the most unforgettable feeling of being a normal human being again. When looking out to the ocean with my feet on land, I knew what fear was. I then realized that the supernatural power that enabled us to survive on the ship had left me, and I resumed being a simple girl. Wondering how I had managed to do what I did, I would shiver with fear. I was so scared of the ocean and was deeply moved that God had saved my life.

I was, after all, an ordinary teenager who could feel the overwhelming shock and aftershock of such an incredible experience. That was a miracle!

Today, there is a debate about how America should deal with refugees from Syria and around the world. Between the political or religious points of view, I simply agree with the requirements of screening, checking, verifying, and confirming the backgrounds, histories, and sponsorships as thoroughly as possible, for the sake of this country's security. The misguided interpretation of hospitality that dictates we open our arms to receive the needy homeless without any screening is like opening our home or country to unknown thieves or killers.

Rose's Principle #8: Seize the Moment

Do what you believe in with your heart and might and believe that the divine power is with you, especially when you are in danger. I did. I did not let my fear stop me when I knew what I wanted. Could it be that I was so influenced by my father's character of bravery and gut that I, too, reacted in much the same way he did? I'm sort of, "like father, like daughter."

Let the strength of your personality grow and embrace it without reservation or hesitation. Live your life so that the fear of death can never enter your heart. When you arise in the morning, give thanks for your food and the joy of living. And if perchance you see no reason for giving thanks, rest assured the fault is in yourself.

I carried all those memories with me without recognizing that the fire of hope for a better future also existed in me.

Exercise Action Steps:

Be alert to your surroundings. Notice what's there? Light, color, sound, smell, texture, temperature, sunny or windy?

Take it all in. Savor it. Pause when something draws you in. Notice it deeply, but without judging its usefulness, beauty, or appropriateness. Simply allow it to be whatever it is.

Notice *now*. Observe totally with gratitude. Believe that wherever you are, whatever experience you may encounter, it is meant to be for a reason. You may not know the reason now, but eventually, you will understand how all the pieces of the puzzle fit together. Just be grateful and thankful that you are there and alive, no matter how it might seem to be in the moment. Keep the fire of hope burning, but do not neglect to be fully in the present. Be truly alive!

9

New Life in a New Land

On August 2, 1976, I arrived in California to a new life and new opportunities. The weather, people, and multi-cultured spirit made me feel tremendously grateful for my new home. Looking out the window in Mission Viejo, the phoenix inside me rose to greet the new world, ready to move forward, full of energy. With a sense of urgency to catch up from over a year of lost time under communist rule, I wanted to jump right in with a new learning program.

With some help, I registered at Saddleback Junior College, a two-year college, to study music. I took some general education courses, staying after class to copy notes from classmates or talking to the teachers for details that I missed during the lecture. My English wasn't very good at the time, but, due to my French background, I progressed rapidly.

I worked very hard, wanting to make what my parents had gone through, giving up everything they had for my future, worthwhile.

My younger sisters and brother were going to high school and helping the family after school by working a subcontracting job in soldering for my aunt's company. My parents and I cleaned big office buildings, in addition to the wiring and soldering we did at home

Once I went to college, my parents encouraged me to concentrate on my education and told me not to work on splitting wires anymore. That was when I turned to piano tutoring and private piano teaching, besides weekend church organ playing, to earn money. After that, I was also introduced to a job as a Vietnamese interpreter by a very good friend of the family. I became one of the first Vietnamese Certified Court Interpreters in the Orange County courts.

I made good money as an interpreter while going to college, majoring in piano performance, and pursuing my passion in classical piano. I didn't foresee the future. The reality was that the money earned as a private piano teacher in classical music, even with a Bachelor of Music Performance, was not enough for me. I eked out a living and was unhappy. My parents slaved away day and night.

My father tried hard to come up with some creative business ideas, but, due to the language barrier, he struggled a lot. He invented an amazing manual machine to cut multiple wires all at once, without having to use scissors and cut the wires one by one. It was regrettable that none of us knew anything about filing a patent for his invention.

He also invented some whitening facial cream for Asian skin and produced the product for the market, but, without the proper marketing and funding, he didn't succeed as expected. After his initial creation, this product became popular when some other people with more financial backing picked it up.

My father always strove for better. Creative, dexterous, and very hard working, he was willing to sacrifice himself to improve his family's lot.

I wanted desperately to be able to provide a better life for him, but I was helpless to achieve that. I kept trying, but there was nothing much I could have done at that time, except for being a busy, good student and a good girl.

My piano teacher, Mrs. Chai Nakyong, an exceptionally talented Korean pianist, happened to be a head of the Music Department. She helped me discover my inner self through my piano playing. I remember her complimenting my fast fingering and good technique, but she'd scold me, "Don't you have any feeling, any expression?" I could whip out Bach and Mozart flawlessly, but nothing in the romantic style. My playing had no expression, no emotion. I could not express it. The burdens of that time weighed heavily on me and affected my playing. After having gone through all this trauma in life, facing death and fear of the unknown of the future, my heart was "frozen." Cold and indifferent, I wondered how I could move on without knowing who I really was inside.

At the end of the two-year period at Saddleback, I transferred to Cal State University of Fullerton, majoring in Piano Performance. I used to practice at least five to six hours a day, any time between and after classes. I didn't even consider what the reality would be in pursuing a classical piano career. Blindly, I poured myself and my passion into the piano without thinking ahead of what the future would bring.

I no longer lived at home, but I carried a feeling of responsibility and obligation to pay back and help my family.

One day, I locked myself in an attic of the Christian dormitory and read a book by John Powell called *Fully Human, Fully Alive: A New Life through a New Vision*. This book changed my life. I realized I was putting too much pressure on myself. Feeling behind in my education and my growth due to all I had been through in the recent past, as well as becoming acquainted with my life in a new world, I was left scrabbling to make up for it.

The pressure I put on myself to pay my parents back for their great sacrifices resulted in me trying too hard to keep up and bottling up my emotions. I was afraid of being a regular woman. Instead, I acted like a machine, putting forth constant, intense effort. I felt guilty when I took a break. I was always on the go. I was never able to relax or allow myself to enjoy or fully live as I should.

Upon reading Powell's book, I realized that I wasn't truly living my life. It was such a relief to learn that I could live fully and completely, instead of living like a machine. With this revelation, my frozen heart melted into unstoppable tears, and I sobbed for hours.

The recognition that pain, struggle, strife, and hardship are the ingredients of a life well-lived overwhelmed me. I had survived the worst in the ocean. Could anything else be as scary?

I thought not.

So, after years of only half living, I allowed myself to breathe and feel more of my own music.

It wasn't easy at first. Learning how to relax was new for me, and acknowledging how hard I had been on myself helped. I consciously allowed myself to slow down a bit. I even began to accept invitations to go out for fun.

Then, I got a chance to earn some supplemental money by tutoring piano and playing the pipe organ on Sunday masses at the Old Mission Church in San Juan Capistrano. (It's one of the great landmarks for tourism in the world.) How was I so lucky to be part of this historical church and environment? How blessed was I to be doing that and getting paid for it? The kind and generous Father Paul Martin believed in me. I didn't think I was good enough at playing the organ to get paid, but I was so grateful for that supplemental income I didn't realize that I was an entrepreneur even then.

After graduating with my Bachelor of Music degree, I served as a volunteer, playing the piano and the organ for the

Vietnamese choir at St. Nicholas Church for quite a few years after I moved back to Laguna Hills.

~ ~ ~

Reflections: Know Who You Are

It was important for me to try to figure out who I was and why I could not express my feelings in my piano playing. By contemplating my frozen state at the time, I could face what really had happened in my life, so I could either make a change for the better or be defeated by the circumstances. I chose to take a "new me through a new vision" approach. It was a process of self-awareness, self-understanding, and self-appropriation.

I paid attention to how to express my feelings at the keyboard, not only with finger technique but also with gaining sincere awareness of my true feelings. I learned to let emotions out without reservation, like I had done years before. Of course, I could not let go of all my reservations at once, but this step, awareness, is the key to a new perspective in life.

Soon, I could feel and I could share without fear. I could start to live in unity with others in a social context. I could dare to step out from my own island. When we become more fully aware that our success is due in large measure to the loyalty, helpfulness, and encouragement we have received from others, our desire grows to pass on similar gifts. Gratitude spurs us on to prove ourselves worthy of what others have done for us. The spirit of gratitude is a powerful energizer.

Rose's Principle #9: Be True to Yourself

After a lot of thought about my teacher's remarks, I read and tried to understand why I bottled up all my emotions. I took my courage in hand and faced the problem to find a solution.

I cried a lot, but I didn't stop there. My fear of the unknown had made me believe that my emotions had to remain frozen. Now, I decided to live fully and listen to my heart. I felt such a great relief that I could be myself, without being judged or criticized by rigid cultural rules and public opinions.

For example, for the first time, I could wear a mini skirt and be proud of my beautiful legs. In America, this was no big deal; in my culture, however, this could cause negative comments. I learned that my value as a person didn't diminish because of some old conservative, narrow-minded judgment of how long or short a skirt should be. It has little to do with actual morals or respectable conduct.

I still tried to balance between the mind (reason) and the heart, so I wouldn't later regret basing a decision solely on emotion. At least, I recognized that I needed to listen to my feelings and find the freedom to express them. After all, I risked my life for freedom and human rights. I learned how to think carefully and determine when to hold back and when to let go; to combine the good and the bad of both eastern and western cultures, and, most of all, to be true to myself.

Exercise Action Steps:

1. Stand for what is right and just, for good and not evil.

2. Examine your conscience and choose to do the right thing and hold strong to integrity, truth, and honor.

3. Follow the Golden Rule: "Do unto others as you would have them do unto you."

4. Be compassionate and empathize by putting yourself in the other person's shoes so you know how they feel.

5. Pray for guidance from the Holy Spirit or apply the basic commandments from the Christian Bible or the book of good spirit.

10

Code of Honor

In the summer of 1979, I transferred from California State University of Fullerton to UCLA. My original assigned Korean roommate was switched to a Vietnamese roommate after orientation. During that time, I was teaching private piano lessons for extra money. I happened to be teaching this family with two boys. The father was an American who spoke Vietnamese fluently and had worked for the American Embassy in South Vietnam before the war was ended. He married a Vietnamese woman who was a friend of my aunt. One day, a young Vietnamese man came over to borrow some Vietnamese Confucius books from this American man. How ironic that was! Unbeknownst to me, this young man saw me teaching piano to the kids.

One day, this young man was there when I was showing pictures of the homecoming queen event at CSUF to the lady of the house. We were introduced casually, but I didn't think anything of it, as I had decided not to date or get involved with men. Not long after, while I was on the freeway driving to UCLA, I noticed that a Mustang kept following me. Like James Bond, I sped up and slowed down, trying to lose it. When it came close to an exit to get off, the driver looked at me, smiled, and nodded his head respectfully to say goodbye. I didn't recognize him at the time. Thereafter, my roommate told me that through a conversation she had with her brother, they both discovered that I was the girl teaching piano that he'd met, and he was the same man who followed me on the freeway. Knowing that I was a music major, he asked my roommate to invite me to go to a concert with him.

I agreed to go on the condition that we would double date. However, at the last minute, there were only two tickets left, and only he and I went. How did that happen? Even today, I still don't know the real reason.

He'd attended the seminary of La Salle Institute in Vietnam to become a Christian brother, specializing in education. His goal was to teach and train the students to be better leaders for the government and the country. His dream was big but was broken when he was airlifted out of Vietnam five days before the South's fall.

After our first date, he pursued me madly. I kept my distance, insisting on being just friends, testing his character. He was very honest, sincere, patient, considerate, thoughtful, and mostly generous. Soft-spoken and well-mannered, he was a true gentleman.

When I said that I wanted a room to teach piano privately, this man built an additional unit behind my parents' house all by himself. During the construction, his finger was accidentally nailed, but he continued to build that room with one hand. This really touched me. This proved to me that he loved me and would do anything for me.

I had already prayed for God's guidance in choosing my life partner. To me, marriage was a lifetime commitment and one of the most critical decisions I could make, so the qualifications of my future husband had to include honesty and high morality. Wealth would have been nice, but it wasn't as important as the other factors!

Believe it or not, I had tested his patience, his honesty, his integrity, his mind, and his heart in many ways. After four years and prayers for wisdom and guidance, I accepted his proposal

We got engaged in November of 1983 and married in April of 1984. After that summer at UCLA, I returned to CSUF to finish my Bachelor degree in Piano Performance because UCLA was stronger in musicology than piano performance. Looking back at that summer, I wonder if fate had guided me to the man who became my husband later.

Marriage is sacred. There were other men who chased me, among them, one who claimed to be madly in love with me and even cut himself to show me how desperately he wanted me to marry him. I searched myself, knowing what I wanted and what my priorities should be. I wanted to have an honorable and happy family where I could achieve my goals to repay the debts I felt I'd accrued over my sometimes chaotic past. I used my head more than my heart and made sure to follow my instinct, my gut feeling when it came to trusting a man or acknowledging a man's vices, weaknesses, and qualities. I valued myself highly and would not open up my "kimono" easily.

I not only played hard to get; in fact, I *was* hard to get and proud of it. I refused to fall for the lies or infatuations of some men. It wasn't easy for me to trust men, and I wouldn't sleep with any of them because I respected myself too much to let that happen. I was proud that the man wasn't allowed to hang up the phone before I did. That was me.

The Phoenix Rose, after all, had overcome death to be where I was. I couldn't shame or disgrace myself or my parents. Self-respect and earning respect from my future husband was a necessity in my code of honor.

My husband pursued me for five years before we got married. I think he should earn a medal for patience! I had declared to his family early on not to expect me to be a traditional, submissive daughter-in-law. My mom had been a mistreated daughter-in-law, and I swore I wouldn't follow in her footsteps.

I could write a book about this phase of my life and the struggles with the in-laws. Their antiquated Confucian belief that requires the husband cleave to his family, instead of his wife, has ruined many marriages and destroyed many families. How I escaped it could be an educational course for both older and younger generations to learn from and to prevent more unfair "suffocation."

~ ~ ~

Reflections

Have you carefully evaluated the person you've decided to commit to, based on their moral values? How about their family background and educational level? Have you taken the time to verify what they say and who they really are? Do you trust them on sight, or do you need to verify their truthfulness regarding finances, ego, or their need to control? Have you observed how they react when they don't like what you say or when you disagree? Are they honest and respectful, or are they opinionated and narrow-minded? Or are you only looking at their appearance?

You need to pay attention to the differences between you and acknowledge if any conflict you encounter is tolerable or unreasonable.

It is important that you don't accept any disrespect, verbally or physically. Don't put up with frivolous behavior. Trust your sixth sense. Choose your beliefs; choose your standards; choose your thinking; choose your being. Stand responsible for your own destiny and your own happiness in your life. Phoenix Rose = Will Power and Goals. Besides the will of the mind, our heart needs to flame with the fire of love for self and others.

We live, we err, and we progress. But it's wiser to learn from other people's mistakes!

Rose's Principle #10: Self-Control

Honor yourself enough to have inner self-control and self-respect. Do not give yourself easily to any man. The consequence for a moment of lust is not worth the loss of respect and trust of a sacred relationship in marriage.

As human beings, we have our natural animal sexual instinct and desire, but we must resist and wait. Wait for the right person and wait for the right time. This is different for every person, accordingly to their own principles and values. However, to me, it is wise to honor oneself and not throw oneself away too easily.

Just imagine, if you are craving the main dish, and you get to have it all at once, are you sure you want to have it again, or do you walk away to look for another dish? However, if you are only given small bites of appetizers and not the main course, you'll naturally crave the main course...but you need to wait for it.

I think it is important to wait and only give out some appetizers in very small bites, even to your chosen man. Time teaches us a lot of things. These lessons help us reap a happy future or suffer the consequences of our own stupidity.

Perhaps I'm old-fashioned, but there's a price for everything. Resisting momentary pleasure for honor, long-term respect, and trust is worth everything.

It is a great lesson to learn and great to train yourself to exercise this self-control. By doing so, you honor yourself.

This self-control can be applied to other weaknesses, such as eating, spending, gossiping, cursing, drinking, and more.

Mastering self-control makes a huge difference in your life. It is the art of masculinity and femininity combined at the appropriate timing and circumstance. It creates the law of attraction with honor and wisdom.

Exercise Action Steps:

1. Respect yourself as a precious son or daughter of your loving parents.

2. Value yourself as an honorable person who deserves the best life can offer.

3. Train your willpower daily with small challenges, such as resisting sweet candy or chocolate; not ditching class to go to a party fulfilling your duties instead of neglecting your homework; or doing your appointed tasks instead of wasting time.

4. Repeat the mantra: "I do not sell myself for a cheap price that I will regret." Pride and Honor I must keep.

Pleasure is one thing; wisdom is another. Unbridled, the first leads to sorrow, though pleasant at the time. The latter, though at first unpleasant, leads to lasting joy and happiness.

11

Husband and Wife as Business Partners

My priorities from the beginning of my marriage were always my husband and my children.

Two years after marriage, I had my first son. While my husband worked as an engineer, we started a video rental business in the city of Mission Viejo. This allowed me to be close to my newborn baby, instead of working for someone else. That was the good news.

The bad news was that, as entrepreneurs and first-time business owners, we made multiple mistakes. Location, location, location should be the main factor for success or failure in retail business. It was a huge mistake to have our store on the second floor a few blocks from one of the largest video rental chains, which opened up soon after we did. And we couldn't do much about it: Mission Viejo is a city with many strict regulations—one of which being that we couldn't put a banner in front of our store.

We made nickels and dimes, and it wasn't worth it, and we sold the video rental business. My husband started another business in computers with some people he knew. This lasted for a couple of years, but it also didn't work out. He'd trusted the wrong people.

Near the end of 1989 and the beginning of 1990, we started another business together. (At that point, I was pregnant with my second baby and our oldest son was almost three.) The business was called ASL, Inc., and it was in a 2,000-square-foot office space in Irvine. My second son stayed in my office while my oldest one went to preschool. With one hand, I held the milk bottle and fed my baby, while I held the phone between my ear and shoulder and wrote with my other hand. That's how I used to work and take care of my baby at the same time.

It was natural for me to know what the baby needed, so there was hardly any crying in the office. Before the baby was hungry or when he needed to be changed, I took care of it immediately. I was so thankful that I could be with my baby and still manage the business with my husband.

My husband focused on the technical aspects of our company, while I took care of everything that was non-technical—administration, accounting, marketing, human resources, finances, and sales. I wasn't trained in any of this. I had to read and study along the way. My critical thinking, common sense, and determination carried me through. I strongly believe that there's always a solution to what you want and need to do. Just pray, find it, get it, then do it.

In the beginning of the business, I could only get a credit line of $2,500 with the vendors, but that slowly increased with time until we landed a huge contract. I remember one of the vendor's representatives saying that if he would have known the growth potential of ASL, he would've asked to invest in our stocks.

I created and organized every necessary form for all the departments from scratch and set up all the rules and regulations for our operating procedures. My husband developed a form-fit board, which he called the "transformer board." The invention became our niche in the market. With this board, corporations could upgrade all their different brands of computers to be compatible with each other for one-fourth of the cost of buying a new computer. It was like a smart brain or heart transplant, technically speaking.

The business started in a small warehouse, operating as a manufacturer. I first hired a secretary, then salespeople to sell to corporate accounts, while I studied how to do business with the government as a minority, woman-owned company. es, I was a minority woman who was grateful for such a program and America's outreach consideration

By monitoring the salespeople and creating sales tools with a continuously refined sales pitch, I discovered the way to get the company a huge contract with the government through EDS (Electronic Data Systems), a Ross Perot company.

Besides having my husband's brilliant product invention, how did we win this contract? I must give credit to my genius husband's visionary mind when he made his pricing calculation. He predicted how computer parts would decrease in cost, ahead of time, to make the most incredible offer with pricing none of other bidders could beat.

This made ASL into a $40-million-dollar company within three years of the inception of the business. We grew from our original 2,000 square feet to 4,000 square feet, then 12,000 square feet, then a 32,000-square-foot manufacturing building in less than five years.

At this point, I changed our company's operating system from manual processing to a larger software manufacturing/inventory control system called Material Requirements Planning (MRP). MRP is a production planning, scheduling, and inventory control system used to manage manufacturing processes. This was necessary; it was impossible to handle our large-scale production and high volume by hand at that stage.

While juggling being a mother, a wife, a CEO, , I constantly prayed and searched for guidance and wisdom to grow accordingly without "drowning." There was a continuous struggle balancing the traditional, submissive Asian woman and the outspoken, modern side of me. I had to be aware of and respect my husband's honor. In addition, I had to adjust to the swift growth of the company and delegate prudently. It was extremely hard to let go of my tendency to be a control freak, but I knew I had to. .

The move from controlling most everything to delegating was not easy for me. I still wanted to oversee the end results, but I learned to restructure the operation through my managers and channels of command accordingly. It was great being my own boss, so I had the final say-so. But I did take employee feedback into account, too.

We had agreed from the beginning that my husband would have final say over technical matters in regards to his engineers and development, but I would be the CEO and president who finalized all other matters, including financing, management, and marketing. I handled all legal issues, including contracts and human resource decisions. My husband was too easygoing to do this. I could be firmer and bolder when it came to making hard decisions.

The one mistake I made, and lived to regret, was not taking advantage of lines of credit from banks—even though I didn't need them. The bank usually doesn't loan you what you need when you need it; so, when you don't need it and they offer it, you should consider it.

Our business's extraordinary growth during the recession made headlines all over—*Orange County Register*, *Los Angeles Times*, *Readers' Digest*, *OC Metro*, *International Trade Magazine* and major computer magazines, as well as *Working Woman Magazine* and a TV show called "Making-It Minority Success" on Fox 11 News. We won multiple awards such as Pioneering Woman from National Women Business Association, Entrepreneur of the Year from the Asian Business Association, as well as from Ernst Young, from the Top 500 Corporate Women-Owned Business magazine. Under the name Rose Hwang, I published articles like

"Will to Survive Spurs Success," "Keepers of the Dream," "Survival as the Bottom Line," and "Transferring Life Lessons to the Boardroom."

The power struggle between a typical Asian man and a determined woman was a great challenge for our partnership in business and in marriage. Since it was our own business, we used to bring home business issues 24/7, too. . Our two personalities are so completely opposite. As a result of being trained at a Catholic seminary, my husband is sweet, soft, gentle, patient, and naïve in the sense that the world is all kind and good. I am the opposite—aggressive, positive, firm, suspicious, impatient, and daring.

I usually got what I wanted while allowing him to save face. For example, in the beginning of the business, I was very dissatisfied with the norm that corporations paid their vendors net 30 days but, in fact, did not pay until 60 or 90 days later. I told my husband that I wanted to ask the corporations to pay earlier than net 30 days. He told me that it would be impossible to convince big corporations to change that norm. However, I wouldn't take "No" for an answer. I insisted on finding a way.

I discovered these companies could get some points with the government for giving favors and support to small minority businesses. So, I asked for a favor they could perform: with a little persistence, I got a special exception of net fifteen and net ten days instead.

This really made a big difference in the beginning of our small business, allowing for better cash flow and faster accounts receivable conversion. I learned that nothing is impossible if you really believe in it and it is communicated to the right ears or channels. Just do not give in to the norm, even if the majority does it. There is always a possibility or an exception.

Here, the phoenix rose tremendously, to the heights of being a millionaire at age 34. This seemed unreal.

I used to take a walk with my husband around our neighborhood in Aliso Viejo to nearby Nellie Gail Ranch, where I saw and was amazed by huge mansions. I wished to live in a similar mansion. Sure enough, in November of 1993, we bought our mansion in Nellie Gail Ranch, over 7,000 square feet of equestrian estate on an acre of land.

Was that considered a miracle? Yes, I think so. Was this dream pre-meditated? Yes, it was. I wished for it. My husband and I achieved our goal and our wish together. What a blessing! As Napoleon Hill once said, "Whatever your mind can conceive and believe, your mind can achieve."

My dream had come true. I could take care of my parents, who lived with us. This, however, was a two-edged sword.

My father suffered with multiple health issues resulting from the hardships in his life, including the stress of our escape, but, most of all, from losing his golden past failing to overcome the language barrier and build his new life in a foreign country. It was heartbreaking to see him suffer with arthritis, osteoporosis, lung cancer, mental depression, and the struggle of not being able to build his own empire as he had done before.

This proved to me that mental stress is deadly in itself. We need to learn to choose our mindset for a better outcome in life. Thinking of one's past glory and being unable to let go to accept the present can kill you faster than you can imagine.

I remember a time when my father was so stressed that he was a ten-pack-a-day smoker, with sleepless nights of thinking and scheming about how to rise again. He turned into an old, white-haired man overnight. Watching it tormented me, but it also made me want to work harder to be successful so I could ease his pain and grief. I empathized with him, knowing that he felt helpless. He desperately wished to help the family members he'd left behind in Vietnam. He'd been a man used to supporting all his brothers' families, but now he lived with sorrow and suffering because he no longer could.

From our point of view, of course, he shouldn't have thought less of himself for not being able to do what he couldn't afford. But that was easier said than done. He was a self-made, successful man who had endured much to be a generous brother and friend to many people. He had even contributed to many hospitals and orphanages without telling us. (I didn't know of his generosity until after he passed away and we found thank-you certificates from all those places.) At last, he came to the place where he could let go of his guilt, and he accepted the reality that he couldn't do all of this anymore because of his circumstances.

Another major reason for my father's short life was my mother's resentment and unconscious revenge for his playboy past. She distanced herself from him and wouldn't put up with the hot temper of a now helpless, lost man. He sank into insecurity and an inferiority complex that accelerated his deteriorating health condition.

It was sad to see this. These were two unchangeable adults who held onto their old griefs and grudges without a way out. My mom stayed on for the sake of her children, even though the marriage was not a happy one. Their example taught me to treasure and nurture my marriage through better communication. I didn't want to repeat my parents' marriage suffering.

So, while being tremendously successful was good for me, my husband, and our growing family, it also had its difficulties and distractions: negotiating interference by my in-laws and the power struggle between husband and wife were just two of them.

~ ~ ~

Reflections

What do you do when you're in conflict with your spouse?

With age, a relationship may not be the same as it was in the beginning. There will be times when you can feel hurt, misunderstood, misjudged, unappreciated, or abused (verbally and emotionally). When you are down and depressed, then, what are you going to do?

It seems two people, no matter how deep their love, cannot live in constant harmony. Mistrust and misunderstandings appear inevitable, for we feel betrayed when the other does not behave in accordance with our conceptions of love and loyalty. Thus, we cannot live in perpetual peace with one another, something I desperately want to be untrue.

Sometimes, you wonder how mistreatment can happen to you, how is it possible to hear heartless words from your most loving spouse, how angry you can feel because of those nasty, mean words, and sometimes how cold and distant you may become toward your other half.

As for me, I truly believed that the ugly part revealed was not truly my husband's nature. . I reminded myself to fight against the trap of feeling like a victim. I also prayed fervently to hold onto my basic belief that my husband did not really mean to hurt me, that he might be suffering himself with some insecurities or struggles. I gave him some space and some time to reconsider his doings and sayings, knowing that he would come back from his cave in time.

In these tough times, I would remind myself to remember his qualities and virtues, to learn to forgive his shortcomings and inconsideration. It was not easy to do, but I would not give up a sacred marriage and a family for my pride or ego. Humility and honor sometimes seem to conflict with each other, but for the sake of the unity of a family, it is worth to choose humility over blind self-honor. It may be considered a self-sacrificial act, but it is a choice to make for a worthwhile reason and cause.

Anything can happen in life. Just face it and deal with it. However, remember that sin is a refusal of responsibility. It creates division, alienation, dissension, marginalization, and rejection; sin "dis-members" the body. When stress may be the cause of exhaustion and conflict, as husband and wife, father and mother, we can take a rest and recharge. But don't give up, for responsibility is called for here, not selfishness or excuses.

I'm proud of being loved and honored by my husband for many years, especially during the early decade after marriage, despite conflicts between my in-laws that affected my husband's love for me. I held up strongly and kept faith in my husband's love and dedication to me and his children. I was confident of my uniqueness as a woman of beauty and virtue. I took pride in having a moral, loving, dedicated, faithful man in my life. The more you have, the more painful when it is less than you want or expect. It has been over 32 years of marriage, and it is getting really challenging with the ups and downs, with the repeated arguments and disagreements and the two opposite levels of energy of two individuals are taking its course.

After many years of marriage, how many of you still wonder a bit about your husband's love? Granted that my husband is a faithful and highly moral man, why do I feel so hurt and angry when I hear negative words from him? He'll say things like, "I'm tired, I give up. Why are you so difficult to work with? Why are you making me feel weak?" (This one happened when he was comparing the firmness of my muscles with his out-of-shape body.) Sometimes it feels like competition and jealousy, in business or in social situations. We can be two completely opposite characters, one a dreamer and one a realistic fighter.

Sometimes, sour conflicts seem childish, and the tension seems ridiculous. I never thought this could happen to me. I used to hear, "There's no more fun after the honeymoon." But I was so certain that none of that could happen to me, such a wonderful woman as I am.

Guess what? It is just life, and the waves never stand still or stop until we die. The question is, what should I do when I feel beat up mentally, too? What should I feel? Hatred? Resentment? Surrender? Should I give in? Let it flow? Or give up?

I vow that marriage is sacred, and I will keep my oath of loyalty, integrity, and faithfulness. But it can be challenging when love is worn out, and it seems harder to tolerate our extreme differences.

There were times when I felt much dislike toward my partner when he showed what I saw as indifference and a light-hearted attitude through his words and lack of energy. I felt taken for granted so constantly in so many ways, in almost everything I did, said, or believed. Is this how love and marriage should be? I doubt that. What should I do when I feel so suffocated and unhappy, but the obligation to stay and find a solution still remains?

Rose's Principle # 11: There Is Always a Solution

Whenever we are in turmoil, we worry that our happiness is over. But life has ups and downs. When we encounter tribulations, it is time to lift our head above water to breathe and look for a positive solution. Do not drown yourself in your dark tunnel, but open your eyes and ears to a message from your guardian angel.

Have faith and pray for a solution. There is always a solution, if you keep your mind open for a positive and constructive one.

When a possibility occurs to you, take it, if it won't hurt anyone in any way. You never know; something good may happen instead. We attended retreats and found several positive support groups to help us figure out our problems and find ways to solve them.

When we find the right people in God's way, solutions can only help us to see the light that we couldn't see before.

Keep learning and open your mind to see the light. Be ready to take your stand for the right cause, love over despair.

Again, when we feel disappointed in each other, we may feel tired and worn out. Pray for the tidal wave to come down, but do not give up or start handing out ultimatums. For as long as the fire of hope is burning, have faith in the positive qualities in each other and wait.

Exercise Action Steps:

"During the episode of a breakdown in connectedness, a breakdown in trust which is the essence of negative insanity, each suffers in isolation feelings of betrayal. When caught in this, please help us, Lord, to not add to the fire of destructiveness, help us to rise above our ocean of negativity and realize the immense suffering of the other. This is true love and is the essence of servitude to one another." This is when you should remember to feel the "Phoenix Rose" with the Fire of Hope in your heart and take these practical steps:

1. Control your mindset by doing the breathing exercise we mentioned earlier (breathe in for four counts, hold it for four counts, exhale out for four counts), while tightening your core muscle until you feel you are in control of yourself.

2. Calm yourself in prayer and silence, even in solitude.

3. Read or write. Journal events and feelings on the right side and leave the left side blank for later review.

4. Take charge of yourself by telling yourself: "This family or my life can be heaven or hell. It depends on me." Decide for heaven and be willing to humble yourself for love.

5. Find the right time to communicate with clarity.

6. Set priorities right and focus on the goal. In my case, my priority is to thrive to recover financial loss and remind my husband of our main target, which is to put our differences aside during our efforts to rebuild our success or financial growth. It is compared to the metaphor of two soldiers with different personalities who must stand by each other and watch each other's back for survival purposes to prevent being killed by the enemies in a battle. United we

live; divided we lose, whether in war, business, or our emotional lives.

7. This requires another session by itself. Everything has two sides, the positive and the negative. We must make a choice, and that is when our mindset can make a difference in the outcome. Choose wisely; even though you feel with the heart, choose with your head and pray for the wisdom to do it right. Sometimes, to lose is to win….but with respect. Be responsible for your own happiness.

12

Overcoming Conflict with Love

*I*n the Asian culture, wives, especially those supported by their husbands, were required to be submissive to the in-laws and were controlled by their in-laws' influence over their son. Men were taught to put their mother before their wife. For this reason, a submissive wife was highly sought after, as this showed she would respect her husband's parents and obey them as tradition demanded.

Thus, a husband rarely stood up for his wife. Sometimes, this led to abuse. The son's wife was expected to make unfair sacrifices and often became a servant with no avenue of escape. Most women were forced to tolerate it, as it would be immoral (or at least unacceptable) for a wife or a daughter-in-law to express any objection to any of the demands or the expectation of obedience put on them by their in-laws.

Today, of course, most women are no longer able to tolerate such discrimination and unfair treatment, especially those who are self-sufficient and capable.

I cannot accept this tradition, especially with what I experienced in my childhood, watching my mother's mistreatment and suffering. Why should a wife have to compete with her mother-in-law?

Asian men were also expected to support and repay their parents and family members. If they didn't, they felt immoral and guilty. This particularly fell upon the oldest son, and it's an obligation that caused many families to fall apart.

Now, my husband is the oldest son and was expected to take care of his siblings and mother by sharing his wealth. (After his father was killed by the communists when he was six, his mom was treated like a queen.)

My in-laws had no interest in us in the beginning, but, suddenly, after our company's growth and the public attention, they wanted to influence my husband's position and control over me. His unemployed brother and his mother said things like, "Blood is thicker than water," and "There is only one mother, but wives can be replaced like a piece of clothing." Out of jealousy, they urged him to take charge of the entire company and remove me as CEO. They hoped to make me a regular housewife, without any rights or control.

They also wanted more financial support from him and tried to make him feel guilty for not fulfilling his obligations as a dutiful son. I resented their interference, and my husband was torn between us.

I was distressed and unhappy. How would you feel if your in-laws said this? Would you be angry and bitter? I was. It was suffocating.

Not surprisingly, my husband and I argued and had problems we'd never had before.

It's not right for a man to be put in this position, squeezed between two opposing factors like a sandwich to be eaten from both sides. I resented it and felt betrayed at first, although I tried to understand his reasoning. In our culture, there was nothing wrong with how much he loved his mother and siblings.

But they went far beyond what was acceptable. They urged him to do things for them behind my back. They knew exactly what to say to make him feel like my position of power within the company made him less of a man. They picked away at his ego until he felt threatened by me. They wanted him to exclude me from my rights as a business partner and contributor to our success and growth. Then, he could fulfill their expectation of sharing his financial wealth with them, without my consent. They didn't want me to have any say in what they wanted my husband to give them as his payback.

His mother expected us at every weekend event she had. Since California is larger than most distances between cities in Vietnam, it was not a matter of "get up and go," especially with little children. It took a lot of energy and time to spend every weekend with his mom and relatives, even if it was for fun and to create lasting bonds. It was impractical. When his siblings made insinuations designed to create division and doubt between my husband and me, it created more heartache. It might have been unintentional and maybe I was overly sensitive person, but I couldn't ignore how it affected my husband. Was it because I was insecure after having a few babies or because my policy was to prevent, instead of to cure, if possible? I was also aware that this type of interference was a bad habit of most large Vietnamese families.

Torn between wanting to please my husband and his duties to please his family and the urge to protect myself, I struggled. It was challenging to deal with while running a business, taking care of my children, and trying to save my marriage.

At some point, I realized that my defense strategy wasn't working, especially when I was up against his siblings and, mainly, his mother.

At times, I felt like a single fighter standing against a large army. It was frustrating and horrible. The struggle to prove my innocence against every false accusation caused our relationship to harden and grow cold. I wrote journals of my pleadings, feelings, and self-evaluation and let my husband read if we were too upset to talk.

With all of this going on, I still wanted to trust him, not be suspicious of him because of his family and their agenda. I worried about what his family wanted from him and what they would do to get it. And, yet, I was expected to love his family as much as he did, be quiet, and not oppose them in any way.

Their machinations began to interfere with our business. We wasted time and energy on unnecessary fights, stalling important business decisions.

I guess I wasn't a traditional woman in that sense. I couldn't tolerate it. I told my mother-in-law that if she expected my husband to consider me invisible in his financial decisions or contributions to any third party, then that would be treating me as if I didn't exist. Torn between being generous and protecting myself, I didn't want to commit a sin, even in thoughts and feelings.

People change with the change of status. Sometimes, their change stems from outer influence and, sometimes, from their egos. For my husband, it was both.

Over 32 years of marriage is the essence of a journey that spans up hills and downhills, goals achieved, unexpected joys, and times of failure, disappointments, and offenses that sought forgiveness. Chapter 13 of the book of Corinthians is a discipline and a constant for the days and years. Love is not arrogant or rude, love glories not in one's ego or being right, love suffers and is kind, love hangs in there. And ultimately this delicate, gentle but tough bond supersedes all else and becomes the one imperishable gift we can have if we are humble enough to receive it.

In that spirit, I asked God to help increase my compassion so that I might rise above my anger and resentments. I was consumed with my own self-importance—that without me, my husband could not have succeeded. How long would I continue to be trapped in my self-centered, destructive ways of perceiving the actions of others?

Too often, I feel I'm the victim who has been treated unfairly and, therefore, cannot be at peace. How long will I feel betrayed? How long will I feel insulted? How long will I fear domination? How long will I feel disrespected and invalidated—by deed, by word, by tone, by facial expression?

"I begged God for the gift of not perceiving the negating of my reality, the insult, the domination, the disrespect, the betrayal, the unfairness: to allow me to truly feel the fear, the hurt, the vulnerability, the feelings of being overwhelmed in the other. I trusted that I could have that compassion, and yet I did not have to allow myself to be taken advantage of.

"If this gift was not given to me, I would be eternally consumed by my fears, my insecurities, and my fearfulness. Please God, give me the gift of compassion for those who insult me, hurt me, disrespect me, betray me, ignore me, and treat me unfairly...

"Without God's mercy, I will forever be a prisoner within the dark dungeon of myself filled with fear and anger. So, Lord Jesus, please save me from me. I am thankful for the adversity which has prostrated me before you. I am thankful to be reminded of my powerlessness, and thus awakened to you and to my own self. I have been drowning in a sea of self-created, self-centered turmoil, submerged in thoughts of painful darkness, unable to maintain a resting place upon the mountaintop of perspective and peace...

"I am confronted by my old enemy of desiring to hurt another who has been an impetus for my anxieties. I co-create my problem but refuse to face myself and take responsibility, even though I'm given brief glimpses of what I've really done. Oh, God, I beg for humility to admit my imperfections and to clearly see how I cause harm by resisting against my husband's generosity. If I'm not given this gift, I will die in the hellish darkness of blaming others for my victimization... Over and over, I destroy myself. I truly want to punish people for my feeling wronged by them... I seek help from

Jesus, to please help me take responsibility for how I co-create the difficulty. I seek compassion for myself and for the others, my in-laws, so I can resolve to deal kindly and firmly with the problem. Oh, God, let me have compassion for who I am and not anger at others for betraying me, for taking advantage of me.

"Let me rather simply and quietly protect myself, forgive, and continue undisturbed to give thanks for my good fortune of life.

"A harsh word, the perception of a promise broken, a feeling of being abandoned or betrayed, destroys—for some period of time—the feeling of closeness and connection of love and trust. It can happen suddenly, no matter how close two people are, no matter how long they've known each other. Then the question becomes: 'Will we be close again? Will we trust each other once more? And if so, how long will it take?' When trust is forgotten, it is easier to enter episodes of negative insanity, repeating to ourselves and others all the bad the other has done to us, repeating to ourselves all the hurtful things we feel we want to say and do.

"Then the question becomes: 'Will we really say and do those things? Or will we remember our love and rise above ourselves?' When feeling love, love is real. Nothing else exists, not anger, not hatred nor resentment...

"When feeling angry, anger is real and love does not seem to exist... Is not love the context and anger but a short burst within it? Is not love as the sun, always there and anger but as a passing cloud?

"Destructive, angry thoughts invade me; each is a reminder of past humiliations, disrespect, and injustices. I am totally consumed with a frown that pervades my entire self; my eyes look like clouds with no inner light to be felt. I cannot resolve my problem with the other person; I feel repeatedly violated and unable to forget or transcend it by compassion or wider perspective, for I am too trapped in darkness to remember love... A sea of negativity has truly engulfed me...

"Only by God's grace can I remember what it is like to smile, to forgive, to feel the simple holiness of human dignity. I cannot see beauty nor feel the innocence of a child. The limit of what I can endure from another seems to have been passed, and I am lost. Now, I am a disturbed wife haunted by memories and visions of feeling violated...."

Until May of 1999, my husband and I attended separate retreats, one for men and another for women, called Cursillo. This retreat was designed to bring you closer to God and to help you become evangelists. Two months after attending Cursillo, we happened to go to another one. This second retreat, Marriage Family Enrichment Retreat, is where we reconciled. The conflicts caused by my in-laws, their insinuations, manipulation, and accusations were resolved.

Even though the Marriage Family Enrichment Retreat had helped us tremendously, the problem originated from tradition and couldn't be cured overnight. Fortunately, we met an older couple who became our counselors and godparents and helped us out of this vicious circle.

Amazingly, with God's grace, my husband learned to put his priorities in order and avoid any unnecessary guilt caused by the differences between Confucius and Biblical teaching.

Once he reset his priorities accordingly to the Bible's teaching of Ephesians 5:31, "*Therefore a man shall leave his father and mother and hold fast to his wife, and the two shall become one flesh,*" he could make peace with himself and the fact that he had to prioritize his responsibilities for his own family first.

I always write down my thoughts, my feelings, my analysis, my reasoning, my beliefs, and my pleadings with facts and logic when I don't know what to do, until I find the answer or the solution. I set the time to have a one-on-one talk with my husband to make sure that whatever misunderstanding or unresolved issue is dealt with consciously and seriously.

We set some rules for ourselves—such as during any disagreement or dispute, under no circumstance is one of us to leave the house and drive away. Either one of us may go to the backyard or to another room, if necessary. Just not off the premises entirely. We learned we could argue, disagree, then make up and make love after sincerely apologizing and resolving the issue. We reminded each other that we loved each other and reminisced about how hard he pursued my heart and hands, so I could feel that I was his number-one priority, as I always expected to be.

I make him a priority, too: I care for his feelings, his needs, his concerns, his worries, and don't allow any interference from anyone outside our relationship, including direct family members. Since I made this very clear, after a while, no one dared to interfere because I believe that I know who I am and I trust my husband.

Sometimes, I felt stressed because life was full of ups and downs. Then I always reminded myself not to hold his hurtful words to heart. Accordingly to John Gray's book, *Men are Mars, Women are from Venus*, men usually don't mean what they say and forget easily. It's wise overall not to let words crush you or to play the emotional ping-pong game, especially in anger or distress. (It took me using some mind control to do that!)

It took lots of reading, learning, praying, and consulting with the right ears and wisdom to obtain my own control of inner peace. It's just normal that there are sunny, windy, rainy, foggy, cloudy, even stormy, days in any relationship. However strong our foundation of trust and commitment is, we can learn to overcome those moody days and feelings without throwing in the towel every time we might disagree.

Whatever path we tread will at times be a difficult way. It is within the difficulty that the seeker finds, for a moment, the brilliant jewel of the true self. Instead of fighting against my in-laws' large family and defending myself, I decided to focus on building a strong relationship between my husband and me through sincere communication and clearly stating my feelings and needs. Whether my husband was convinced of my true heart toward him and his family and my efforts to work out any misunderstanding and hard feelings, my attempts at self-defense or self-protection caused me to suffer greatly. It was a vicious cycle—the more you're hit, the more you get hurt. I finally reversed my strategy and stopped fighting. Instead, I focused on accepting any possible financial losses that might happen and put more value on our lasting relationship and the peace of my family. After all, all I did mainly was to fight for our marriage and our family's happiness and the future of our children.

I have prayed for the wisdom of forgiveness to wash away the wrongs of all I see that was done against me. It was through the grace of God that I found peace so I could continue to keep harmony in my family. I learned to understand and accept my in-laws for who they were, knowing that I couldn't change them. Finally, they know to leave us alone and are on good terms with me. I am grateful that all of them, especially my mother-in-law, have become very friendly and kind to me. We loved each other more by giving each other our rightful space.

By altering my thinking and choosing compassion, I could finally overcome the conflict. Because of that choice, we empathize with each other and trust each other again.

~ ~ ~

Reflections

When conflict comes into your marriage, how do you maintain harmony and balance?

Value what matters, and do not let money blind your judgment. Money can come and go. However, marriage is sacred. It needs to be nurtured and honored with love, communication, compassion, and forgiveness.

If you are in search of your true love and happiness, there must be some way to obtain what you wish for. The challenge doesn't stop there. You need to have a formula to keep it and maintain it once you have achieved it, especially in a relationship. In silence and solitude, you will come to meet the Beloved of your heart. For silence is power, the power of the Divine Lover blessing and transforming you.

This is an ongoing learning process and hard work Learn and understand how to deal with inevitable changes wisely and with kindness to sustain a lasting and loving relationship.

Rose's Principle #12: Self-Empowerment

To empower myself, I had to know who I was and what I wanted. I knew that I wanted to be loved and cherished by my husband and didn't want to have to compete with his mom for my position in his affections.

I knew that I respected his struggle of being squeezed between his mom and me. I didn't want to accept the traditional role of the wife who sacrifices her wishes and life to her husband's family.

My focus was to have better communication with my husband in the face of any misunderstanding or accusation from his family members. It was up to me to build a trust and love so strong with my husband that he'd be my protector, instead of my having to fight alone against the whole army of his immediate family members. I had to know my position and strengthen our relationship with a sincere and kind heart.

Exercise Action Steps:

By knowing who I was and what I wanted, I empowered myself and was not the victimized, silent daughter-in-law tradition dictated.

I then prayed to God to show me how to accept the conflict without injuring my opponents, yet still win the love and trust of my husband.

This can be the same for you. By knowing who you are and what you want, you become empowered. Once you know, you need to come from a place of love. This will empower you without disempowering others, and you will retain your self-respect. Imagine life is like an ocean with tidal waves where you are water, the most powerful and resilient substance which does not break. Keep flowing, keep doing your duties to keep the family alive, in silence if necessary, but don't give up on your sacred marriage.

Realizing that the differences between how men are stimulated—mainly by visual outlook—and women react to audio input, I would need to remind my husband how I felt hurt when certain words could affect my feelings and behavior. It is important to remind each other how we feel or are affected by certain silly habits or circumstances.

In the early years of courtship and relationship, we felt love with our hearts. In the later years of our relationship, it would be our brains that felt love. So be aware that harsh and cruel words can kill love. It became the unique wedding of head and heart, thinking and loving. So, holding our tongue and not verbalizing inconsiderate or regrettable thoughts and words helped keep our flame of love burning.

13

Balancing Parenting, Business, and Life

O ur business has brought us comfort and luxury. After we sold ASL in 2005, my husband started another enterprise, and I withdrew from business to become a full-time mother. My three sons were nineteen, fifteen, and twelve years old at the time. They attended private schools and had been taken care of by my mother, who followed the schedules I gave her. Now, I took over my mom's job as their full-time chauffeur. The challenge of balancing parenting, business, and life took on a new meaning. I found myself navigating new, unchartered waters, since being a full-time mother for my two youngest sons could be considered a late start. I felt nervous, like I had finally arrived at the station just before I would have missed the train. There were times when I had to stop the car during driving to seriously address misbehavior by my youngest son. I wanted to understand his reasoning in these incidents, so I could help him recognize the facts objectively and either make corrections and amendments or at least learn right from wrong, while feeling loved and cared for. When I was upset at his wrongdoing, I wanted to confirm that I was upset at what he'd done, but not at him as a person. I wanted him to believe that I had faith in him wanting to be good, for when you know you are given time to repent and know that you are loved and believed in, you tend to feel guilty and try to be good or better. It is the fire of love that produces the fire of hope for better results.

Transitions

The transition from CEO of a business to a full-time mother and chauffeur was difficult for me. I had mixed feelings. On one hand, I had the privilege of being close to my children; on the other, there was the challenge of running around like a chicken with its head cut off because of the schedules and responsibilities.

Yet, I was grateful that I could be there for my sons during their teenage period. I was blessed to follow my sons' after-school activities and be present when they had issues. I have always been the mediator between my sons and my husband.

Thank God my oldest was such a sweetheart and well-behaved. During his last three years of high school, he worked full-time every summer at our company, learning all aspects of the business, going from assembly to computer technology to administration to sales and customer service. Later, when he was attending college full-time, he became a full-time manager.

The Art of Listening and Decision Making

I wasn't a patient person, but I consciously paid attention to how each of my children felt and tried not to jump to conclusions about a situation without collecting all the facts and clarifying them with my sons. However, I did teach them right from wrong, reviewed the daily Bible verse they learned from school, and helped them analyze the facts of a circumstance, while letting them make the final decision. For example, my oldest son told me that he was bullied by some boys at school. They would take his backpack and throw his books out on the floor.

After getting all the details from my son, I advised him to tell the bully he'd no longer tolerate his behavior and the next time it happened, he'd report it to the office. If my son gave him proper warning and the bully persisted in harassing him, then I encouraged my son to take a stand. Should the boy strike him three times, he could respond in kind, but he had to make sure he didn't injure his opponent. He was only to do enough to get his point across and to stop any more bullying. Since my son had taken private Kung Fu lessons for his protection, he knew how to do this. He followed my advice, and that boy stopped bullying him.

No physical force is necessary unless it is in self-defense.

My kids played hockey in a neighborhood cul-de-sac. There was friction with some other boys. One day, one of my sons ran into the house in tears, upset at one of the other boys. I listened to his story, asked him questions, and elicited his own solutions on how to handle the situation.

He asked me to go out and yell at the offender. I refused. I couldn't always be there to protect him, and he had to learn how to solve these problems. I presented some options for him to consider. Was the matter worth fighting for? Could it be resolved amicably by talking it out or just walking away? Did it need to be brought to a parent? Or should it be resolved with force? If so, could he win or not? Did he care to continue to have this person as his friend or not? He needed to think about how to deal with this problem and find the wisest and most peaceful way to handle it.

He had to learn to make his own decision and be responsible for co-creating his reality and problems. He had to be aware of the pros and cons before acting. After talking with me, he cooled off and realized that Mom wouldn't jump to his protection. Later, I found out that he didn't make a big fuss out of it, and the matter seemed to be frivolous and insignificant after all.

Through instances like these, I trained my boys to use their own judgment, to know themselves, to fear God, and to obey the law. I trusted their sense of right and wrong because I taught them to think logically and be wise.

Listening carefully and respectfully to my children ensured that I had a close relationship with them. Also, I always kept my promise of either reward or punishment. I can't remember how it started, but my children rarely let me count to three. While I was firm, I also did it with love.

If I had to give one a swat on the butt, I always explained why. This allowed them to accept their punishment without resentment. I also made sure that I punished the wrongdoing and not the child. And, after the punishment, I hugged him lovingly to let him know that what I did was out of love and meant to teach him there were consequences for one's actions. It takes lots of energy and time to elicit the facts, acknowledge the feelings, and discover the circumstance before deciding which action to take.

I also strove to ensure there were no misunderstandings or hard feelings for any incident. If there were, I apologized and sincerely asked for forgiveness from my sons. It is so important to me that my son is aware of my passion and desire to be a caring mother. I want to understand his thoughts, feelings, wishes, arguments, struggles, worries, his likes, his dislikes, etc.

When he was frustrated and told me that I didn't listen enough, I took his comment seriously and asked him to repeat what I hadn't truly heard or understood. This way, I clearly knew what he wanted to convey.

I told him that it would break my heart if he felt misunderstood, and I didn't have the chance to correct it. I made sure he knew I respected him, whether we agreed or not.

Communication and Mediation

Communication with my son is extremely important to me. No matter how busy I am, I will never brush him off. This applies to all my sons, no matter how old they are. Even though it takes more energy and time to clear up a misunderstanding, it needs to be done without delay to prevent further regrets or heartaches. It is important to be a good listener to our children's sharing, no matter how small the feelings may seem.

Verbalizations of sentiments like "Get out of my house" create a negative overtone in the house. No matter their age, we should never say such things to our kids. Teenagers often act irrationally. They're naturally impulsive. As parents and adults, we should be more mature to help them avoid doing anything they'll later regret.

Once, one of my teenagers broke curfew and disagreed with my husband about the consequences. He was upset and acted rebelliously by talking back. My husband lost his temper and kicked him out of the house. (Fathers are often short-tempered and bossy toward their kids. They expect obedience.) Their argument was intense, and emotions ran high. I talked to my son and listened to him, then I did the same with my husband. By doing this, I could convince them to reconsider their behaviors and think about what had just happened.

By focusing on bringing positive energy to every situation, no matter how depressed or serious a situation might be, I reminded everyone how important forgiveness and love are in a family.

We prayed together; we stayed together.

We try not to forget how to rise up from our own ashes of anger, selfishness, ego, misunderstanding, or any other negativity. Love conquers all. At times, other people will disappoint you. But that doesn't mean you must to disappoint in return.

In some cases, people will frustrate you with their recklessness and irritate you with their thoughtlessness. The best response is not to respond in kind, but, instead, with love.

You may have the opportunity to lead your life and help lead others in a more positive direction. It takes strength and maturity, but you can do it.

Imagine transforming a confrontational situation into one of cooperation and mutual respect. Imagine being the person who does that and how quietly satisfying it feels.

You can't resolve every conflict, but neglecting opportunities to work through differences in a peaceful and productive way is foolish.

See if you can swallow your disappointment and irritation and look instead for ways to bring positive energy to negative situations. Chances are, you'll make the difference and make things better.

Doing Your Best for Your Children

As a working mother, even though I tried to give my children the best education and plenty of extra-curricular courses and tutoring, I found everything I did wasn't enough to get my kids into Ivy League or other top universities.

The process of getting into a prestigious university in the States is tricky. There was more competition among the elites from the private schools. I learned much later in life from a reliable source that a higher grade from a public high school gave a student a better chance of acceptance into universities than the average percentile grade from a private high school. I didn't know this when I sent my sons to private school. And, even though they were honor students with high GPAs, they weren't straight A students in high school.

My ignorance didn't help my children achieve as high as they could have. As a parent who always wants their children to excel and realize their fullest potential, this failing has haunted me.

To be honest, I believe I had a subconscious reason not to push my kids too hard in school, too. My father's best friend had a son who migrated to Germany from our refugee camp and died of pneumonia when he was 20 years old. I was heartbroken when I heard that news. I could feel his parents' pain. I wanted my sons to live a happy life, not necessarily a successful doctor's life, like most Asian parents wish for their kids. I reminded myself not to force my children to become what I wanted them to be, but for them to find their own path and passion. Of course, there are some who follow their parents' wishes and become happy doctors, but there are multiple cases of those who end up in mental hospitals due to the excessive pressure from their parents.

Earning PhDs or become diplomats or world leaders was not what our sons wanted, and I decided to make peace with their choices. As long as they live in faith and continue to excel in a godly way, I am gratefully there for them, for my philosophy is to respect their choice of life and happiness. I want them to live their own paths, make their own choices, and find their own passions.

We sent them to Christian and Catholic schools, and they turned out to be wonderful children and equally wonderful adults. They have entrepreneurial blood in them and are the best children any parent would wish for, and I am very proud of them.

Having your priorities in the right place means focusing your positive energy for your own sanity and peace—not trying to control others, even if you might feel on one level that it's your right to do so with your children.

~ ~ ~

Reflections

Who and what are the most important things to you? Your family relationships, or what outsiders think? Have you disciplined your children with love, patience, and respect, or out of anger and ego? Many women put their children as their priority and end up neglecting their husbands, which leads to marriage problems.

In my world, the most important people are my spouse and children.

Will you let your son be kicked out by his angry father, or do you have the guts to take charge of the situation with respect and grace? Do you speak with love and patience when addressing your family members so you can talk sense into each one of them and restore peace?

Forgiveness can be given, and hugs can be applied with empathy and gratitude.

If you're in a negative situation, what steps have you taken to help reverse it? Do not give up, but find counsel from the right moral, experienced people.

Rose's Principle #13: Balance of Mind, Body, and Soul

The biggest mistake I made in America was losing millions of dollars in real estate. Knowing how hard it would be to recover monetarily, I suffered and tormented myself. There were nights when I could not sleep, regretful and angry about my bad decisions.

Just like anyone else, I wanted to cry and was upset. How did I come through this all to thrive again?

It was a matter of balancing my mind, body, and soul by living this main principle: prioritize the importance of my soul (faith in God), the control of my mind (mental peace over destructive power), and body (fitness and health).

I was raised in wealth from childhood; I experienced a loss of privileges after the fall of South Vietnam; I dealt with having nothing when coming to the USA; I embraced success in business and the wealth of being a self-made millionaire, which had given me plenty of rewards in life. I am always grateful for all these blessings, hardships, and challenges. I am grateful for my family and that they love me for who I am and not for what I have.

But it is this mind, body, and soul balance that is of the utmost importance. With harmony of mind, body, and spirit, I can recognize the logistical gaps or unmet needs that can prevent good things from happening, and I will personally do whatever it takes to solve the problem and meet the needs. This is the power that helps me overcome any adversity and rise again.

Exercise Action Steps:

Any time in life, especially when you are in desolation instead of consolation, remember not to make a change or issue or act on any ultimatums. It is time to be the water that flows with the waves. Meditate and breathe in the positive energy, focus on what there is to be grateful for instead of the negative, and remember the beautiful memories that make your heart warm. Keep that fire of hope burning for the better.

When at a conflict in a relationship, even when you may feel hopeless, disappointed, or hurt:

Do not play the ping-pong game, throwing ugly and mean words back to your adversary in the moment.

Put yourself in the other's person shoes to hear and understand what could be misinterpreted and misunderstood.

Pray for wisdom and peace.

Send a sincere text message stating how you feel without using the word "you."

Take some time out to read, meditate, think, and let out your feelings by confiding in a trustworthy counselor.

Wait for an opportunity to communicate in a civilized, calm, and respectful way.

Trust in God for a resolution. Have faith in yourself and in your loved one.

14

Human Weakness in Social Groups

Have you ever been hurt by a social group? Have you ever been misunderstood and "crucified" in some way?

The communists didn't hurt me through betrayal; they only terrified me. Another factor in that time period actually gave me grief and significant pain. By now, you know that I will stand up for a good cause, especially for justice. In 2008, there was a major crisis in a social and religious program in which I was an active member and a volunteer.

By accident, I found out that some key members of a program planned to betray its founder to boost their own statuses and egos. The plan was to take over all the intellectual property from its original creator by changing just the name, then passing it over to a different clan.

I was shocked and puzzled. So, I initiated an investigation and a petition campaign and conducted a mission to see justice done.

I tried to help the rightful owner of the program recover the damages from being betrayed by his most trusted initial followers. It wasn't a pleasant situation, but I felt obligated to help clear up the misunderstanding between the parties with the hope of preventing the unfair takeover.

The worst pain wasn't that I had to fight for what I believed in, nor the time I spent for it while running my own business, but the misjudgment and betrayal of a few members from the temporary team after the problem was solved. After being able to regain the lost position and lost rights of the program, I was criticized for being too aggressive and too bold during the fight; they ignored how much I had sacrificed in time and energy to achieve the results. After it was accomplished, people on the temporary team changed their tune and pushed me out of the leadership position.

Since my mission was accomplished, I stepped back and let them run it. How ironic was it that people criticized me once the war was over? Do people not understand that tactics used when you are at war are different from when you are in peace? When the house is on fire, you must take immediate action to stop the fire. You can't hesitate and follow regular due process, or the house will burn down.

A leader must take action with conviction without wasting time wondering what to do, how to do it, or waiting for approval from others when under an emergency or crisis. So, I was the leader who took the initiative to lead the fight for justice.

The program has had its own challenges and mistakes due to the new inexperienced management, but it has survived the crisis and managed to grow. It wasn't necessary for me to shine in any position of the program, so I accepted being the shadow for the bigger cause.

I could not believe how cruel and power-hungry some people can be. The betrayal and misjudgment hurt, but I prayed to forgive those who had caused me pain and asked Jesus for strength and peace to accept and trust in God completely despite it all.

I heard that this kind of turmoil happens in many groups, whether they were religious or not. It is just human weakness. The ego craves fame and power. That craving will drive people to betray others. It was sad to see this happen in a group I'd trusted.

The one thing that helped me through this pain was looking at the cross and remembering how Jesus was sinless, but He was crucified by jealous and heartless people. So, I, as an imperfect human being, shouldn't expect otherwise.

Arrogance, fame, and ego have caused much of the war and suffering in life. Prayers taught me to forgive those people and let go of any resentment or pain to find peace. The phoenix in me rose from my own ashes of disappointment, hurt, and resentment and took me from victim to victor. With great relief, I felt compassion for those who wanted to hurt me, whether intentionally or unintentionally.

It is up to me to decide if I let others control my feelings and peace or whether I should take charge of them. I had to believe that, in God's time, the truth would come out. And, eight years later, it did.

The new leaders of the program learned what happened to me and came to me, seeking advice on how to handle this challenge.

Good versus bad is just the law of nature. There is peace within for those who fear God and endeavor to rise up from their own wrong desires or motives. It took a lot of courage for me to share this issue; I had to accept my own shortcomings to grow into a better leader and a better Christian, one who takes full responsibility of co-creating any hardship or headache.

I need to learn to improve my lack of patience, my lack of diplomacy in dealing with volunteers, to recognize people's ambition and desire for power, and to accept people can be of different minds, even though we may be fighting for the same cause. Even siblings may not think or feel the same as each other, much less people of different families and backgrounds. I realize that my impatient character—something that's earned me the nickname "Mrs. Now"!—is a double-edged sword. Granted, my aggressiveness and impatience has achieved many things, but I still need to learn to trust in the process.

We can hope for the best and keep trying to do our part through better communication and service. Rest assured, though, you won't always meet with satisfaction and approval from everyone involved. That just won't happen. I did what I believed needed to be done at the time, and I was at peace with what I did for a good cause. That was enough. I just had to let go of any hard feelings, and I was glad I could reach that stage without wasting too much of my time and energy on negativity.

Thank you, God, for helping me rise up from agony.

~ ~ ~

Reflections

Have you ever felt disappointed with people in your religious group or your circle of friends?

It helps at times like that to look at Jesus on his cross and recognize the sorrow and pain He went through. If Jesus, who was sinless, was still betrayed and crucified, then I, a human being with imperfections and flaws, must live and learn and not suffer from some dissatisfying outcome caused by someone else.

I could make the choice to let go of the resentment and disappointment and move forward with peace … or not. So, I decided to be positive and rise above, just like the Phoenix Rose should do. I decided to keep the fire of love and hope lit, instead of the fire of hatred.

I'm grateful for the power of my mind, and the healing power of the Holy Spirit to make me whole again.

My father used to remind me that the tolerance to be wait needs time and patience. I will grind my teeth if I must, but I will hang in there and trust in the outcome.

Rose's Principle # 14: Let Go!

After all the ups and downs, the hardships and the success, the pain and the joy, the gifts and the losses, the struggle and the victory, I am grateful for it all.

I choose what to keep and what to let go. Letting go of any unpleasant or negative feelings from people or situations is the best gift I can give myself. I don't have to carry the load of rotten potatoes in my mind, my chest, or on my shoulders. This makes room for the positive, constructive elements to come forward.

A holistic spirituality has an inner experience of God and an outward expression in relationships. It is part of the process of being conformed to the image of God for the sake of others. It became a systematic method for me to achieve the spiritual growth that centers on the process of conversion.

By letting go, I learned from my mistakes and about my weaknesses, without letting them destroy me. I'm not attached to things that don't give value to the peace of mind and the honor that I live by.

Exercise Action Steps:

1. Listen to all criticisms, comments, and remarks, to extract what you can for self-improvement. There is no need to take them personally because the objective is to be open-minded, to listen, and to evaluate things objectively. It is the same tenacity required in practicing a sport, work-out exercise, hiking trip, or any physical endurance test. Be thick-skinned to work toward the objective, instead of being embarrassed and giving up.

2. Pay attention to your common tendencies of character, such as being aggressive, over-obsessive, over-anguish, impatient, bossy, extreme, hot-tempered, too soft-hearted, or too fast.

3. Do not feel down or depressed when you discover such things in yourself, but trust in your own heart and mind who you are and where you want to be.

4. Learn to recognize your weaknesses or strengths and accept them objectively.

5. Meditate and learn how you can be at peace with yourself. Read self-help books for insights. Different thinking brings different outcomes.

6. Get a mentor who can help. Do not feel that you are alone, and do believe that nothing is too ugly or too shameful to talk about. Unless it is talked about, nothing will change. So be brave and honest with yourself. Deal with it to resolve it.

15

Self-examination

Despite everything I'd gone through, I never realized how important having a purpose was—I guess because I'd always had one. As a young child, my purpose was to learn as much as I could and become a highly educated, successful person who made my parents proud. After the fall of Saigon, my goal shifted to escaping Vietnam. Once we reached the US, I worked to catch up with everyone else and not just survive, but succeed. Once my husband and I had achieved success, I turned all my attention to my children.

But it wasn't enough.

Sometime during those years of being a full-time mother, I lost myself but didn't realize it. Still unaware of what drove me to do it, I got into real estate investments...and lost millions. Inexperience and Hurricane Katrina were hard taskmasters.

Losing so much money overnight wreaked havoc on my pride and heart, and life slowed down for me. I waded through a morass of guilt and shame and struggled to accept it and move on. Only through forgiveness and letting go, believing that once one door was closed, many others opened, could I move forward.

Then, the market crashed. We nearly lost our house, and only through the grace of God did we get through. Was it faith that saved me? I believe it was, and my gratitude to God for rescuing me yet again knows no bounds.

Amidst all of this, I developed an addiction to something I never thought possible: Korean dramas. I loved watching all these dramas on my iPad, sometimes overnight or through the morning. I liked the release of tears and enjoyed the romances between the actors and actresses. The inspiring stories lifted me up with their first-class luxury, success, and cultures.

There were days I regretted losing sleep, when I'd drag myself through every hour, but this didn't deter me. The next day, I was back to watching the shows. After one particularly bad day, I realized it was time to do something about this addiction.

Cutting the cord and not watching them altogether wasn't easy, but it had to be done for the sake of myself and my family.

Coming back to reality grounded me and returned my focus to where it needed to be. Sleeping through the night restored my energy and my will to thrive. The phoenix was rising, rather than living with regret and guilt.

Motivated once again, at the end of 2014, I joined eWomenNetwork and started networking. It was there that the source of my depression was revealed: as much as I loved taking care of my sons, I craved the challenge of business. Although taking care of my sons was very important, I had lost myself by becoming a full-time mom. Who was I? Why was I here? Learning new technology and keeping up with the times invigorated me. So, I attended a weekend conference in Arizona with Sharon Lechter's tribe to get back in touch and begin the process of getting up to date on what I'd missed.

Surrounded by all these confident, highly successful, and non-superficial people, I was humbled and inspired. I felt very blessed to be there. This event gave me hope that I could pull myself out of the depression I'd fallen into. Then, I met Clint Arthur. He encouraged me to share my story and taught me how to open doors for television appearances.

Suddenly, I had a purpose again. My experiences could help others, and I could give back to a country, and the world, that has given me so much. My eye for style, the desire to improve our lives and the environment, my story of survival against all odds—all three of these passions offered me many ways to improve the world in which I live.

This urge to change the world in a positive way not only burns in me but in my family as well. We've been so blessed in our lives, and we want to share this beautiful life with others. So, my husband, my son, and I have created BellaVieNetwork.com.

Bella Vie Network connects vendors and buyers and non-profit organizations. It provides a way to purchase ethical organic and "green" products in different categories—beauty care to health supplements, spice and seasoning to gourmet food, household care, and oral health—from brand-name companies, including but not limited to Honest Co., Nature's Secret, Quest Bars, and Tom's of Maine. We also offer services, such as merchant accounts, solar installation, and event promotions. Members can refer others and earn extra money through their referral fees, while knowing they are helping the world.

Originally designed to help busy moms make extra money without taking too much time away from their children, it's now available for anyone to join. In general, most of the people who live paycheck-to-paycheck need to earn extra money to make ends meet or have something saved for rainy days. This is a way for people to improve their lives and the lives of others.

My ambition is alive again, but now it holds a deeper realization to make a bigger difference in the world. I am passionate about being a messenger and sharing my faith—a faith that has saved me through every step of my life—with the world. I want to help women rise up from their own ashes and transform from victim to victor, no matter what situation they are in, no matter where they may be, or in whatever culture. For where there is faith, there is a miracle. For where there is faith, the fire of hope sustains, and the amazing force of faith pulls the wings of the phoenix up, no matter what state it was in. My passion to do justice was to have steadfast love which would connect to three relationships: to God, to people, and to earth.

~ ~ ~

Reflections

Life goes, no matter how we choose to live it. I have continuously tried to live better, despite the ups and downs, happinesses and sorrows, successes and failures.

Every night, I reexamine myself, recognize my strengths and weaknesses, my talents and my shortcomings, and align them with the principles that give me peace, pride, humility, and thrills.

I remind myself that living is like a wave. It goes up and down as nature dictates. Since our moods and behaviors can change constantly, I learn to be more patient with everyone around me, with less expectation and more flow.

I wonder if I have found my ultimate purpose in life. I know I keep trying. However, there may still be a real calling to come. I just need to listen to the grace of God and be aware of what is coming along my journey.

Rose's Principle #15: Keep Your Eyes and Ears Open!

Upon reviewing the past and the present we benefit from learning from our mistakes, recognizing the gifts we should be grateful for, and acknowledging where we need to improve.

If you just stand still without making any progress or change, you might as well go backwards. Be wise. Keep your eyes and ears open and be alert to what's going on around you, so you can continue to truly be alive by keeping the fire of love and hope burning. Look outside your comfort zone. Recognize your burning concerns. The earth is the Lord's and all that is in it (Ps 24:1). As a matter of fact, we need to care enough to see the possibility of any consequence or damage we may inadvertently cause to children, or to nature itself.

For example, we can see that some parents put work and money before their children. The children might not suffer extreme physical abuse, but they are unattended or neglected. The future stability of these children is not very hopeful. Just like we don't always see how many sea creatures and living birds die because of plastic waste and contaminants to the water and the soil, we don't realize the need to protect our common home, the earth. It is our responsibility to be aware of our surroundings.

Find something you can do to help others less fortunate than you and enrich the world by leaving it in a better state than when you started. With the fire of love inside of you, you can always see things in a more compassionate and generous way and discover your purpose in life.

Exercise Action Steps

Examine yourself and what has caused regret in your life. Ask questions and objectively answer them.

1. What habit do I have that may cause conflict with most people?

2. Do I tend to give advice without being asked for it?

3. Am I opinionated, and do I sound disrespectful to the speaker?

4. Am I a good listener?

5. Am I being impatient and not gentle enough to my other half or family members or friends?

6. Am I a dictator?

7. Am I over-confident in what I think or what I assume is correct?

Be honest with yourself and prioritize wisely, without wasting time and energy on insignificant matter.

   Most of all, to have better peace of mind, put yourself in the other person's shoes to determine how you might be the cause of friction or pain, and stop pointing fingers at others.

16

My Mission Revealed

My husband and I joined the Hearts of Charity as helpers and volunteers for two weeks in January 2016. We went on a humanitarian mission trip to Vietnam. This was the first trip where I experienced great hardship. Its impact helped me find my real purpose.

Among the six people in our group, we flew for 16 hours from LAX, with a stop in Incheon International Airport of Korea, before arriving in Ho Chi Minh in South Vietnam.

Since we had packed six full suitcases with medicine, we were worried that we should expect some difficulties at the airport customs check. We split into three groups of two, each group having two suitcases of medicine. We had a $20 bill ready in our passports, bribe money in case any challenge arose about the medicine. We hated having to do that. However, surprisingly, six suitcases of medicine for colds and flu, diarrhea, antibacterial cream, and other medicines went through Customs without a question. We were all surprised but relieved.

The weather was hot and humid. After a couple hours in a van driving to a convent of Dominican nuns, we stayed up all night, dividing the six suitcases of medicine for distribution to the different locations we were going to visit. We then had to go back to the airport to fly to HaiPhong, north of Vietnam, where the weather was about 50° F, humid and damp. Ten locations were on our agenda: we planned to visit lepers, poor and deformed, and minorities in rural areas, where they lacked basic necessities and were considered needy and outcast.

We were constantly on the run from one place to another, either by van, bus, or airplane. In some places, we were driven by motorcycle on narrow dusty roads to get to huts where there were people paralyzed both physically and mentally.

At every location, we were guided by either a Dominican nun or a local priest of the St. Vincent de Paul order. It was pre-arranged to bring a fixed amount of dried food and condiments for the 250 to 300 families at each location. In some places, we also gave the families solar lanterns and food and medicine.

After going on the tour with the Hearts of Charity for a week, my husband and I continued our trip with a couple who support the St. Vincent de Paul order. Their priests are evangelists who sacrifice their lives to help the poor and minorities and train interested young people to follow their footsteps in servitude.

The second part of the trip included a place called Lao Cai Yen Bai, which is close to the Chinese border. It was extremely cold (below zero) and damp. We stayed overnight at this small, poor parish with a very humble wooden chapel. It was raining and foggy most of the day. We had to slog through mud to get anywhere. This surprised me. I didn't expect such freezing weather in Vietnam. The conditions were depressing and unimaginable.

We had the priests purchase thick blankets to distribute to the needy families there. It was so cold that we personally had to borrow blankets for one night while staying in a very humble room with a cement floor, wooden walls, and wooden beds. But as for our welcome? Their hospitality was warm!

The greatest impact this trip made on us was seeing the true love and great sacrifices these young priests and nuns made for forgotten and helpless people. In their own way, these priests and nuns are also "the forgotten people," compared to most of the other places the media choose to highlight, such as Africa or India.

Is there a way to bring more support to these big-hearted priests and nuns so they can be healthy and carry on their great mission of love? There is a great need for so many unfortunate children to receive an education and have basic living conditions so they can become decent human beings. Just as providing better education and training can help prevent prostitution and crime and elevate the standard of living, ensuring they have clean, uncontaminated water could prevent most of the diseases we encountered there. Instead of having to spend money to cure them, we could spend more money on lifting them up, educating them, and helping them live better lives.

Before going to Vietnam, my husband and I happened to discover a portable water filter. If we hadn't brought some with us, we would've contracted giardia and been exposed to the toxins these poor people drink every day. Those filters helped the six people in our charity group tremendously. This affordable filter has been lab tested and certified to remove 99.99 percent of contaminants, such as pesticides, fungicides, viruses and bacteria, heavy metals, and even Agent Orange, a toxin sprayed by the US government during the Vietnam War. (It takes 25 years for 15 percent of Agent Orange to dissipate. At that rate, the area won't be free of this deadly poison until the year 2132.) Innocent people high in the mountains are affected and damaged the most by this spray. Agent Orange radiation, along with other contaminants in the water, is the main cause of the diseases they suffer, including cancer, birth defects, and liver and heart problems, to name a few. Clean, uncontaminated water is one solution that will reduce the risk of contracting these diseases.

The water filter we bought has advanced technology that naturally enhances the pH and makes water more alkaline for a fraction of the cost of other filtration systems, which cost thousands of dollars. It can last up to 200-plus gallons before needing to be replaced. It saved us from experiencing stomach problems and diarrhea, and having to buy expensive bottles of filtered water. (Since reverse-osmosis-filtered water removes everything, including chlorine, bacteria can grow in filtered water if it is exposed to the sun and heat.)

This BellaVieWater filter also cuts down on the use of plastic and helps the environment. Just think how this filter's technology can enhance people's health and hydration, whether it is for Third- or First-World countries.

I believe it is God's will that I found this water solution. Its natural pH alkaline enhancement ability retains the necessary minerals in the water for people in First World countries, but its capability of removing radiation and contaminants for those in Third World countries makes it an amazing solution.

If you want to learn more about this water filter and how it can elevate your family's health, or donate so we can provide them to needy people around the world and prevent birth defects and diseases, go to www.BellaVieWater.com and join me in this mission.

Being in Vietnam, among the fervent priests and nuns and the unfortunates, strengthened my connection to Jesus. It affected me profoundly. So much so, that after returning to California from the trip, I decided to change this book's title from *The Phoenix-Rose* to *The Fire of Hope: From Victim to Victor.*

I believe I have finally found my purpose. I strongly believe that providing financial support for education and clean, potable water can be a powerful way to bring hope and a better future to the unfortunate children and people in needy areas, not just in Vietnam, but right in our backyards in America.

The desire to bring hope to the needy, the outcasts, and those who are willing to sacrifice their youth and lives for others in these deserted places burns inside of me.

I am urging you to join me in this mission to spread the fire of hope. Find your mission and spread that fire of hope.

~ ~ ~

Reflections

Going on this charity mission really opened my eyes. I'm truly grateful that my family and I escaped Vietnam and made a new life in the United States, a country full of kind and loving people. I have lived here for 40 years and truly thought that life in Vietnam would have changed. It hasn't. There is still deep poverty and fear of the government. Corruption is rampant, and getting ahead or trying to better your family's life often results in some type of punishment from the government and suspicion from others.

North Vietnam declared that they liberated the South from the invasion and oppression of the Americans. The truth is that the South turned out to be the liberator for the North, for the northern people never had freedom, wealth, or luxury until they went into the South. What an ironic truth it became!

I was in the process of finishing this book before I took this trip. Seeing and experiencing the suffering, the sacrifice, and the need showed me how truly blessed I was and has changed my life for the better. The desire to help raise these people up through education and health has become my mission. Finding that water filter, seeing how it kept me and others in our group from getting sick, and realizing what it could do for the people in these poor areas was truly a godsend. This could be a vital lifesaving solution for others. With this filter, I can help others be healthier and have a chance at thriving, instead of just surviving.

Because I paid attention to the message from the Holy Spirit and brought those filters, the entire expedition was completely different than it could've been. Now there is a burning desire in me to give these needy people some hope. My admiration of the young priests and nuns who are sacrificing their own youth and lives for others knows no bounds. Their unconditional love for these people is a shining example of the love to be found in Christ.

To offer everything to the Divine is surrender. Simplicity is surrender.

Always remember, no matter how great we are, that there is something greater—the Divine. To be humble is surrender; whatever you do, give it to God with a grateful and humble heart.

Because of this trip, I found hope within myself as I discovered that the world is not completely ugly, after all. The hope that I could help create a better world left me with the question: What can I do to help these priests and nuns so they can stay healthy and continue their mission of servitude? I put all the dots together and realized that the BellaVieWater filter bottles could, and *should*, be one of the immediate solutions for any human being living there. Clean water means fewer diseases.

In the US, one of the most immediate actions to be exercised is to reduce the usage of plastic bottles to save the environment. Do you know that it takes seven liters of water to make one plastic water bottle? It wastes three liters of water to provide one liter of purified water via reverse osmosis filtration.

Do you know that it takes 19 million barrels of oil to produce and transport the 60 billion of plastic bottles sold in the US each year? There are 30 billion bottles in the landfill that could be there for a thousand years. It is time to change that, for us and for future generations. With this filtered water bottle, there will be no more plastic bottles entering our landfills and oceans.

Right after returning home from the trip, I appeared on a couple of TV shows—these were already pre-scheduled—where I announced the change of my book title and introduced the water filter we'd discovered.

Was all this a miracle? I strongly believe so. I am God's instrument, and I cannot ignore the message or the discovery of my purpose. I want to be a whole person who is a presence that springs from love and leads to love, not only mind and money, but in flesh and spirit, emotions and passions.

I've come to the realization that there is an overwhelming need for every person on this planet to have this special filtered bottle in their hands to be healthy and safe. Due to the truth that 90 percent of the water we consume is outside of our homes, we need to stay hydrated to stay healthy. Most of us may be walking around dehydrated. We also need to control the acidity of our bodies, because cancerous tissue thrives in acidic and dehydrated cells, whereas healthy tissue is alkaline, accordingly to Dr. Otto Heinrich Warburg, who was awarded a Nobel Prize for discovering The Real Cause of Cancer.

Rose's Principle #16: Observe and Listen

By observing the facts and connecting the dots of what happens around you with the people and circumstances, you can discover your calling or purpose.

Be alert and sensitive. Listen to the Holy Spirit so you can recognize your mission, what needs to be done, and how to do it. You may not achieve great things, but little things can be done with great love and profoundly impact the lives of those you touch. In God, everything is possible. Where there is hope, there is the potential for love. Where this is love, there is hope.

Be the Fire of Hope that can help make a difference in the world.

Exercise Action Steps:

Find your burning desire to keep your flame alive for as long as you may live. Do not give up the drive to be ambitious for the better. The more you receive, the more you can give.

The more wealth I have, the more I can give and help. I was devastated to feel useless and hopeless when I could not help the needy as much as I wished, especially when I was desperate to help my helpless father after we arrived to a new foreign land. I could only hope that one day I could change all that helplessness and achieve my goals. I pushed myself to study hard and keep myself wise and safe so I could accomplish my objective. I know I won't regret holding hard onto my hope, the hope to pay back somewhat for the great sacrifice my father made for my freedom and future.

Do not give up on your dream; I never did. To me, it is a sin to stand still and be over comfortable, because we turn out to be lazy and selfish. When we become selfish, it seems like the world stops evolving, but in fact it is us who stop fully living.

Hold on to the fire of hope because the light is just around the corner. Just a little bit longer and with a little bit more effort, and you will get there. Miracles can always happen, as faith never fails when you believe. The fire of hope will never cease until our last breath.

Prayer opens the heart. Each time we pray, we are connecting with a greater source of energy and we are amplifying that energy. Our gratitude, thanksgiving, for even the smallest gift we have received, allows our heart to open. The more the heart opens, the larger our vision becomes. This prayer, this energy, links us with all the goodness on the planet. Faith is like Wi-Fi; it's invisible, but it has the power to connect you to what you need.

Over 40 years ago, as a boat refugee in the ocean escaping on a quest for freedom, I found every drop of drinkable water precious. Water in my utero has protected the wombs of my children and allowed them to be born healthy as US citizens. Being a California resident all these years, I am aware of the drought and the water shortage and take water conservation into consideration in my daily life.

Along those lines, I gave a speech to my son's fourth-grade classmates, providing a glimpse of my escape as it related to precious water, which left those children with something to remember for life. This was at a private school, St. Margaret

Episcopal, where most of students come from wealthy families. I was touched to hear positive remarks from some of those youngsters who, years later in their teens, still remember my story.

Water has impacted my life in so many ways, and it has found its way back to me as a solution to mankind.

Join me in helping yourself and others. Be the Fire of Hope to make a difference and bring yourself and others the Water of Peace!

Since the same spirit who lights the fire of the saints also fuels the vitality of all creation, then "communion in the holy" includes holy people and a holy world in inter-relationships.

17

A Wish Comes True!

After I came back from our humanitarian trip, I decided to pursue a new business related to alkaline water. However, there was a major hiccup with the owner's personal life, and the water filter manufacturer had an unexpected business crisis that put things on hold. The CEO was overthrown by betrayers within his company, and he lost his place and power. Despite that ugly and painful situation, I was there, supporting him in every way I could. We became very trusted friends and promised to be there for each other, no matter what. I prayed for him to be safe. We talked every day and tried to find a way to solve the unfair crisis together, even though I was not an employee or a close friend of his in any way or shape at the time. I had total faith in him as a good person and lent my ears to his challenge without reservation. I value our friendship, as a friend in need is a friend in deed. I was truly concerned about the future of my new water filter business, which had just barely started before this sudden unexpected interruption. But I was steadfast in my belief and faith that everything would turn around very soon.

Sure enough, after more than two months, the CEO of the water manufacturer returned to his previous position and things started to roll again. I was glad that the major hiccup was resolved.

How and why did these things happen? I always believe that there is a reason for everything and, often, the best result comes from crisis.

The bottom line is that the support and faith we gave this friend during his hardship was greatly appreciated. My husband and I became very close friends with him. He appreciated my husband's passion and creativity in development and my marketing talents. We became business partners who were given exclusivity for international business developments, specifically for the Asian Pacific arena, including Vietnam, Thailand, Lao, Cambodia, Singapore, and more.

Was that a miracle? I think so. It was certainly hard to believe. He was the inventor of the technology, the business master of the patented water filtration technology; he had over 30 lab certifications around the world and a brilliant partner.

I was so thankful that we met and turned out to become valuable friends and business partners. We didn't have to make any investment or fulfill any conditions that a normal partnership would have required. It was purely a good-faith relationship. That was so unreal that sometimes I had to pinch myself to make sure I wasn't dreaming!

Tell me, is that pure luck? Good timing? Fate? God's will? It is all of that. I am glad it happened. That just reaffirms my mission to bring this clean and affordable uncontaminated water solution to the world.

~ ~ ~

Reflections

Again, as I have so often before, I experienced a miracle in my life. I interpret that as meaning it's God's will for me to pursue my new and meaningful purpose related to water. My entire life has been impacted greatly with water and by water, from the escape in the ocean, to different stages in life, to traveling to Third World countries, to meeting the expert and the inventor of the water purification. It all seemed to finally connect.

We all need water to live. But the difference in the quality of drinking water can often determine good or bad living. Recognizing and tasting the differences between organic and non-organic food, wealth and poverty, and peace and stress can make a person grow tremendously.

Fortunately, I have been blessed to have tasted the differences and do appreciate the better parts of life. Seeing, hearing, tasting, and touching what life truly at different levels makes me deeply grateful for what I've gained and/or lost. Having and losing money, fame, relationships, or feelings is a natural part of living. Sometimes, when we are so busy in our own box, we may not realize the missing elements outside of our own world that are sufferings or blessings.

One of my latest friends, Nam Loc, a well-known MC in the Vietnamese entertainment industry and the Vietnamese community in general, shared good news. The final batch of 3,000 Vietnamese refugees who had been stuck in the Philippines for almost 30 years after their escape from the Communism of Vietnam have finally migrated to Canada. Unfortunately, many of them refused to be sent back and committed suicide. Others escaped from the refugee camp to live as illegal aliens, without any hope of the new life they'd once expected. I was stunned. How come I didn't know anything about this?

The answer was simple: I couldn't know about everything going on in the world while I was busy with my own challenges, struggles, and responsibilities. But I felt guilty and wondered if my ignorance of such heartbreaking news was unintentionally selfish. I still wish I would have known, so I could have participated in some way to help the people—an old refugee helping new refugees.

I am so happy for these people who finally found a new home after years of suffering in a strange land. There is hope for them, finally.

This is another reminder of the need for my continuous efforts to work hard, grow, build, and drive for better and more. There were times in this later stage when I felt comfortable and lazy, but not anymore. It is not too late to revive my energy and thrive again.

In mid-September of 2016, I returned after spending twelve days in Vietnam and three days in Singapore. In Singapore, I was fortunate to stay with a Singapore couple who also have a residence in California. I learned so much about how expensive the Singapore standard of living is, but it is safe, highly educated, and disciplined, and their citizenship has high standards. I have visited Singapore many times, but being accompanied by natives, I had met significant people and learn so much more than I could previously.

The cleanness and safety of the country reflect great self-respect and pride. It's hard not to feel admiration when you consider the government's amazing management of people and the pride of the country.

We can learn great lessons from Singapore, a small country which has a lack of many natural resources, but managed to keep growing in wealth and peace regardless—a country that is serious about preventing drug trafficking with death penalties to offender. Thus, the country is safe, clean, and a model for many others.

What are the main factors for this proud status and standing of the country? Could it be thanks to the amazing first prime minister, Mr. Lee Kuan Yew's leadership, ethics, and management? He is such a great model for the West. Are we humble enough to learn from a great model of peace of prosperity? I hope so. It never hurts to learn and grow for the better.

There was so much to learn there that it inspired me. . . It reminded me that we always have room for improvement, whether in business, social justice, or our personal growth. Just Never Ever Give Up (NEGU). With this spirit, we can face any challenge or struggle in life with full force, no matter what happens.

Rose's Principle #17: Notice the View Outside Your Own Box

Granted, we are busy with our own responsibilities and duties every day. We may not have the time or energy to care for anything or anyone other than our own family, making ends meet, or enjoying our own life, but we are not an island ourselves. We need to look around us, outside of our own box of comfort or struggle, because we are not alone.

Is it for safety reasons that we don't take time to know our neighbors? When I was in Singapore for a few days, I got to walk with my friends around the neighborhood and met neighbors who were extremely wealthy but so humble and friendly. One of their mansions is recorded as a historical estate in the collection of best estates in South East Asia.

On this man-made island of Singapore, I saw Rolls-Royces plated in real gold and real gold inside mansions. Those who owned cars, such as an Audi, pay the equivalent of US $5,000 in permit fees each year for ten years, plus the cost of the car and importing it to Singapore, which would cost about $125,000.00 US dollars. That gives you an idea of how expensive it is to own a car there, let alone property. My friends are lucky to have inherited their properties from their grandfather, who had owned the properties on their street, this area is considered to be an "Old Rich" area and freehold estate, unlike new lands which can only have a 99-year ownership. I wonder how people make it in such a highly expensive standard. Yet, as I've witnessed with my own eyes, they obviously do.

Everything is possible. It is just a matter of whether we have the ambition and want to strive for it or not. This can be very dependent on relationships; I am sure those who made it that big could not have done it alone. Their achievements required a circle of relationships. This is a lesson to remember: set your goals, but also set yourself up with a circle of the right people to achieve success, so you can then share and help others.

Exercise Action Steps:

See far ahead of the journey you want to take. Is it because of hardship and daily struggle that so few of us know stories of inheritance and prosperity, like those I heard about in Singapore?

Maybe your generation is not at a level where you may be capable of leaving wealth to your offspring, but at least consider this:

1. Teach your children from a very young age to choose the right networks and build their relationships.

2. Place them at the best schools so they are associated with the right level of highly educated people.

3. Help your children build their circle of good friends by allowing them to spend time with their friends and friends' families. (My son went on a summer trip to Europe with one of his very wealthy good friends and classmates. Experiencing the amazing success of that family influenced and inspired him to become a successful entrepreneur with high ambitions.)

4. Know your children's friends and guide and encourage them accordingly. Respect their privacy, but do not lose

track of their journey and direction. Be there for them with love and respect.

5. Create meetings with worthy people and participate in worthy causes to open your children's eyes and ears to a wide network—because it is not what you know, but it is whom you know, after all. That's reality!

6. Knowing that we are not alone and cannot be an island, we are more open to receiving help and helping others. We become people helping people with love, charity, and humility.

7. Remember that we cannot cover the ski with our own hands; it is too big. We need to learn to adapt to our limitations and capabilities. Grow in faith because nothing is impossible with God.

8. Choose which path you want to take or lead your children to, and plan for it when they are still small and young. Everything can be done. Just keep the fire of hope and go for it with wisdom and support.

18

Afterword

Spread the fire of hope by being a flame of love to care and share!

Hope is what we need
Even Fire can burn it
But turn Fire into Hope
Then Love comes to cope.

Fire, a divine element, represents values that man has always associated with. As in Luke 12:49, "I came to bring fire to the world. I wish it were already burning." Just like the Olympic flame burned permanently on the altars, the fire of hope in our heart underlines the profound connection between our intent and the grace of God in his flame of love. It all boils down to self-love, love of others, and mostly the love of God with gratitude, humility, and faith.

It may be a challenge to keep our flame of love or of hope burning with our weak human natures and multiples waves of life, but that is even more reason to continue to fight to sustain it as long we are still breathing. That is the power and the will for a meaningful life, to journey with faith in God and, in love, to do the right thing.

I strongly believe in miracles and believe they don't happen by accident. For example, recently at West Point Leadership Speakers Academy, where I spoke on the same stage as Lieutenant General Russel Honore and the legendary Apollo 11 astronaut, Buzz Aldrin, my topic was about clean water to save the environment and the world. Coincidentally, General Honore spoke on the same topic on October 9, 2016.

On the bus that morning to the West Point club, one of the speakers asked me if I would consider talking to the General about my amazing water filters. This speaker was a Vietnam veteran who had used the chlorine tablet to disinfect his water during battles. He shared how his soldiers used to make a bet among themselves to see whose insects in their canteen would die first from that tablet. They had to drink that water? You must be kidding. No wonder many of them came back with blocked arteries and had heart attacks.

Even more surprising is that, to this day, the same old thing is still being given to our soldiers. How ridiculous is this? Are we not supposed to be the most advanced country in the world? Aren't we known for technology and invention? I can't understand how this could still be the solution for safe water, especially to our service members, who deserve at least some minimal health protection.

This troubled me greatly. I truly feel obliged to do something. I began wondering—should I contact FEMA or …? Is this my mission impossible to be accomplished? Something is burning inside of me, urging me to do something. Like I did in 1992 when I won a big government contract, I believe I may have a chance to bring our water filter to the government's attention. In doing so, I can continue my mission to bring safe, clean, uncontaminated and chemical-free water to those in Third World countries and those who serve our country.

What will happen from here on is a story that awaits the writing of my next book. For now, I believe that the fire of hope is going to burn, for I have a second chance to fulfill my mission.

God brought this fire to the world, although He wished that our fire was already burning. He surely hopes that it should be the fire of love, even though the world is full of disappointment and disaster and hatred and pain. But when we insist on keeping our fire of hope steady, then our boat of life shall resume to balance on the normal "waves" of life. Once calm resumes, we can sail our boat on our journey of life with confidence, and peace.

Over and over again, I have endured the big waves that could have swallowed and crushed me during my journey in personal relationships, business, and social interactions. But each time, I survive and grow stronger and wiser with the grace of God, lots of praying, and the courage to stand up again. I believe that the fire of hope in me cannot die, unless I die. I must keep it lit just like the Olympic light of fire, which must be on in front of the temple of the gods.

~ ~ ~

Reflections

What is Next?

When I went to speak at West Point, I went with a fire of hope that something good would come out of it, whether for speaking experience or some worthwhile networking. I learned how unique each speaker there was and how unique I am.(I had to stand on a block in order to be tall enough that the audience could see me, otherwise, the microphones were right at my nose level!)

I was the smallest speaker there but had the most unique topic: "Can one single water bottle save your life?"

Can you feel my burning desire in delivering my message to the world? It has become even more critical now that the mass media has brought to our attention that 200,000 Americans are exposed to Chromium-6, a deadly cause of cancer due to contaminated water in our old pipelines, affecting more than 23 states in the US, including the city of Flint, Michigan.

Many people don't want to believe that this would be possible in America. It is real, and it is deadly. Just because we don't see it in front of our eyes, it does not mean that it doesn't happen. How sad this reality is! The water cannot be improved because it is a natural cycle of nature that rain comes down to the earth and evaporates back to the clouds. As this cycle continues, so does the rain, but now it comes down as acid rain. The earth has been intoxicated with so many chemicals and manmade toxic substances that have affected the quality of our water. Water that was once clean is now dangerous, even deadly, to humanity.

Sure, there are multiple companies that sell water filtered through reverses osmosis filtration, but so far, none is government regulated and the water quality is not guaranteed.

I appreciate all efforts toward clean drinking water. However, there is much room for improvement.

This brings me back to my father's invention, which I regret being too young and ignorant to get patented. Then, my husband had the vision of the video compression technology when there was nothing available at the time, and he invented the first video compression technology, which was originally the main technology for video conferencing and surveillance. Again, he did not patent it. I was not an engineer, but I knew after the fact that he should have patented it. Again, I regret not doing it.

Recently, my husband came up with something so brilliant, just like his genius transformer board concept years ago, and invented an upgrade-kit concept for the water filter. This time, I spoke up and said, "We must patent it."

Rose's Principle #18: It is Never Too Late!

Twice I've regretted not applying for a patent—once for my father's invention and once for my humble husband's. Never again.

No matter how simple you think your idea is, if you believe it is unique and universal and after due research find that it does not yet exist elsewhere and will make a difference, take action. Learn from my mistakes. A lesson learned is a lesson gained. I know that it is never too late to learn from mistakes and make corrections.

Do not hesitate. It is only right to claim your right and preserve what it is yours for the good of mankind. Do not underestimate your own creation and contribution. If it is meant to be, it will happen. Just follow your gut and do it. I strongly believe that it is a gift from God, and I will make it happen wisely this time.

I have gone to work immediately searching for a local patent attorney, and I've made an appointment. My intent is that the next empire will be started and run by my three wonderful sons. It is a legacy that they can have the means to help the young missionaries in the world with their evangelization and aid the poor.

It is our second chance to make it again from the passion and belief based on "the more I have, the more I can give," because I want to give and help others. We want to share more of what we have received by the grace of God and the joy of giving. We have learned from all the mistakes we made, and we will do it better this time.

Exercise Action Steps:

1. Review and remember your mistakes were so you can learn from them.

2. It is never too late to make corrections, no matter how old we become or how late our business may be founded.

3. Take the right action when it is necessary and do not delay or procrastinate. No more excuses, either from fear or lack of money. Excuses are no longer acceptable.

4. Believe in yourself and your creation. When it is done for the good of humanity, be grateful and confident in protecting your own invention. Claim your right legally.

5. Do not fear any challenge, because the greatest fear is fear itself. Just trust in God and your own convictions.

6. Spend money when necessary for a good, legal patent. It is worth the investment.

7. File at least a provisional patent and later a non-provisional patent, if possible, worldwide. It may be costly, and it may be wise to measure the pros and cons, but for sure, you must consider it.

8. Remember to ask for a signed non-disclosure from any third party to whom you disclose your invention, even those who you secure to make a sample. You never know when someone you think of only as an innocent bystander might steal your idea from you. It is only wise to take precautions to avoid unfair misuse from others.

19

Why Fire and Water?

*T*his book started with writing my escape and survival story, and it continued with the fire of hope from my own struggles in life, through my humanitarian experiences that finally leads me to the mission of clean water.

Why water? Simple.

Water is the link through my journey on earth, from conception and while I was in my mother's womb, to the surrounding power of the ocean waves when I was risking my life for freedom. Through the waves of marriage, relationships, business challenges, parenting experiences, and the continuous striving for a better living with a meaningful purpose, there has been a theme that has led me to my purpose.

You can relate human behavior to the symbol of fire and the symbol of water. As for myself, I have recognized my hot temper and impatience, like the impetuous nature of fire, during most of the years of my youth. During middle age, I have found myself surprisingly calm, like water. Acquiring the wisdom I needed to apply to my life has had much to do with the observation that the flow of water can shave huge rocks through years, transforming them into tiny pieces of gravel.

The persistence and determination of water is unbreakable. Accordingly to Qi, water represents the invincible strength of wisdom; according to Feng Shui, water represents wealth and peace. From its arrival on earth to the vast areas it traverses before emptying into the sea, water holds all the knowledge and experience it has acquired. As phenomenal as it may seem, water carries its whole history, just as we carry ours. It guides us along a remarkable journey through our planet and continues our work to reveal its sacred value to humankind. Water carries within it our thoughts and prayers. As you are water, because 85 percent of our body is water, no matter where you are, your prayers will be carried to the rest of the world, and you need water to be alive.

We can apply water's wisdom to our own lives, and by learning to respect and appreciate water, we can better confront the challenges that face the twenty-first century.

When you feel like water upon confrontation with any emotional challenge and can keep your calm stature, it is called maturity. It is water of peace, away from friction and confrontation.

So much comes down to one word: water. The ideal result is coming to a state of simplicity. The simple solution is to save the world with clean water solutions, for better overall health of both our people and our planet.

How unpredictable life can be! The fire of hope that has carried me through all my ups and downs has led me to different phases of growth, always in faith that I would survive and make it to the so-called water of peace. The water of health and happiness is important in the abstract form, while the clean water that results from our special filter ionic absorption micron technology is a practical solution to contamination.

Water serves as a reminder to us of living with the most strength in its soft, flexible style and character.

How amazing it can be when we realize what we can do to achieve our goal for the betterment of humanity. Keep flowing and keep living, no matter what. For physical, mental, emotional, and mostly spiritual growth, we must strive to be like the power of water. To be physically safe, we must be aware of the cleanliness of the water we put into our bodies and how peaceful our souls can be. We must live as calmly and righteously as clean water is.

The elements of life include fire, earth, air, and water, but through water, I can accomplish my committed mission to make a change to the earth and the environment. Let's keep the fire of hope that the world will continue to be protected by people who are responsible and care to prevent the earth from losing its healthy ground. We must beware, so in future generations, our children and their children won't suffer from the consequences of their ancestors' ignorance and irresponsibility.

Every flame can light up the darkness. Together, we can be as powerful as water.

The Fire of Hope and The Water of Peace can complete a meaningful journey of youth and aging. That's the beauty of being fully alive and fully human. Accept our fire of passion and our humility like water, so we have no regrets, and so we know that we have tried our best to conquer our fear and make the most of life with the heart of love, compassion, and gratitude. After all, gratitude will bring the peace of water to our souls.

Together, we care and share.

Final Note from the Author

The Phoenix-Rose in the Fire of Hope and the Water of Peace from Victim to Victor is a symbol of ying and yang, power and beauty, toughness and gentleness, and rising out of the danger and the art of blending in with nature. It is a combination of the flow of energy from one source to another, from the will of action to the result of achievement. Each one of us has a gift inside waiting to be discovered, acknowledged, and applied. Awareness of our weaknesses and strengths, our inner peace and struggle, and our good and bad helps us rise above challenges we may face in life. A strong faith in and reliance on the divine power of the Holy Spirit will help us overcome all obstacles. As you open yourself to your soul, a calming sense of peace and connectedness develops within you. This peaceful feeling deepens your levels of thought, releases the innate healing powers of your body, reminds you to be grateful for all the gifts of life, and broadens your perspective, so you can be at peace with the way things are.

Our natural instinct for survival encourages us to "just do it" without hesitation, but we must have a plan or a strategy to achieve our goals. Listen to your "gut" (or the "will" or "action-forward") to achieve your goal. Go for it. When you believe it, your mind can conceive it and you can achieve it. Our takeover of the communist patrol ship proves this.

The phoenix rose out of the danger to go for the rose of freedom. It wasn't just for survival. It was the fire of hope for freedom and family unity that brought in me the courage to overcome and move forward.

As for relationship issues, you can't just "do it." You need to know yourself to know others. Honor yourself and know how to love yourself. Write down your feelings and facts, but also seek counsel. Don't make emotional decisions or any ultimatum out of desperation. That will only result in regrets.

From all the experience I've gained through the years, one thing I've learned is every problem has a solution through faith. It is the answer and an absolute necessity. If you pray for divine help, it will be given.

Sometimes, divine help comes in the form of counseling from others. It's wise to get help from qualified and caring experts, someone who values happy and harmonious living —and with a practical system, such as of the Phoenix Rose Transformational System, which includes combined core values of the Eastern and Western cultures and philosophies, recognizing the elements of life in fire and in water, for balanced, full living.

On December 5, 2015, I had the privilege to speak on the main stage at the Harvard Faculty Club among the international thought leaders of the Business Expert Forum. That was the breakthrough in my speaking career. It confirmed to me that my mission was to deliver the message for which I survived. It was faith that saved me and guided me through every step of my life. The spiritual person is one whose whole being, whose whole life is influenced, guided, and directed by the Spirit that is from God. He does this by infusing into us incredible gifts we could not possibly produce through our own limited human nature.

I champion those who can't stand up for themselves. My mantra is, "No matter what, you can triumph over adversity." I help transform tribulation to victory and help others find the courage to fully live the American Dream with the fire of hope in their heart.

Becoming rich in knowledge and faith will make you a better person and bring you a happier life. Having compassion, without allowing others to take advantage of you, can help you live life fully and wisely. Never give up when the going gets tough, for the sun always shines again after the rain or the storm. Seize the moment here and now with the people you love, appreciate all the blessings with deep gratitude, and live your "Phoenix-Rose" without regret. Be thankful for the thorns, for through them, we have a deeper appreciation for the blessing and beauty of the roses.

Care for yourself physically through healthy nutrition and regular exercise, because you have only one body. To be mentally strong, you must have a healthy body; one depends on the other.

Living happily is an art of living beautifully, healthily, successfully, wisely, and peacefully. It originates from the mind, so you can start taking action now to make a change. You can choose to improve your appearance, your image, or your marriage, relationships, family harmony with your children, or your connections with others. We need to go through a process of being conformed to the image of God for the sake of others. By God's gracious giving, we are commissioned to be channels of grace to one another.

I have never forgotten any of the blessings that I have received. I am grateful for the power I gained from all my hardships. So, I am passionate to share my wisdom to empower women with the self-esteem and confidence to improve the love in their relationships, which strengthens their family happiness and stabilizes the futures of their children. A peaceful family will create peaceful children with better and positive outcomes.

You can add enjoyment and meaning to any task by beginning each one with an awareness of the Divine Presence and by taking a moment of silence to be grateful for all you can do! Even the most difficult or mundane task can be done effortlessly and joyfully when approached with an attitude of thanksgiving. You are open to new creativity, new energy, and new inspiration. While working, focus on the Divine Presence, and see how the day goes by with ease and efficiency...and, too, see how your work is blessed.

My calling to be the Phoenix-Rose is to spread my wings and rise up from any challenge I may encounter; in surviving what I did, I resisted forces that would have pulled me down. I am grateful for being an American, and I hope all of you always remember how blessed and fortunate you are, more than so many people in the Third World countries. To learn to be grateful for each challenge, every heart, every tear, as well as for the unexpected joy and love you encounter, is a lesson of great growth. Even a moment of expressing your gratitude for your own creation, your own eternal life, each day brings you closer to the love and power within.

In all things may we be grateful, our hearts open to joy. O Blessed one, speak to us within our hearts; let your Voice be heard.

As we listen and heed your Word, joy will be our song of thanks and proclamation.

As you lead us into the silence, we become friends with solitude;

With trust in you, our lives become simple, with assurance and peace leaving no room for fear and all that we have is a gift from you, all that we are is yours, as well.

May we come to see that all we give to others, we give to ourselves and you.

Faith can make the impossible possible; the Phoenix-Rose in you will awaken to fly out to your destiny. Keep the fire of hope burning and move toward the water of peace. Rise up in gratitude, and never give up! Do not lose your flame even when you make peace with your pain, for faith is the power to get you through your journey.

ww.BellaVieWater.com

www.RosePhan.com

Email: rose@rosephan.com

Face book: facebook.com/rphan11

Twitter.com/rphan1

Linkedin.com/in/rosehphan

www.BellaVieNetwork.com

www.BVNWellness.com

www.ingramcontent.com/pod-product-compliance
Lightning Source LLC
Chambersburg PA
CBHW072150090426
42740CB00012B/2208